Praise for Wade Rouse's

It's All Relative: Two Families,
34 Holidays and 50 Boxes of Wine

"Damn you, Wade! I missed two eBay auctions and delayed taking my Ambien every night for a week so I could finish *It's All Relative*, but it was so worth it. This book rocks! Charming, funny, and saucy enough to make me blush."

—Laurie Notaro, *New York Times* bestselling author of
We Thought You Would Be Prettier

"Wade Rouse's books combine the one-two punch of hilarity and heart and never cease to delight. Filled with uproarious one-liners and enough soul to truly satisfy, readers are going to clamor for a seat at Rouse's holiday table. I can't tell you how much I loved this book."

—Jen Lancaster, *New York Times* bestselling author of
If You Were Here

"Wade Rouse has officially become the laugh assassin. . . . [His] remembrances of his family holidays are masterfully gift-wrapped in delightful dysfunction and topped with a bow of laser-sharp sentimental insight designed to help you not only laugh at but also fall in love again with your own jacked-up gene pool. This book is the gift that keeps on giving."

—Josh Kilmer-Purcell, star of *The Fabulous Beekman Boys* and
New York Times bestselling author of *The Bucolic Plague*

continued . . .

Praise for Wade Rouse's Memoir
At Least in the City Someone Would Hear Me Scream:
Misadventures in Search of the Simple Life
A *Today* Show Summer Must Read

"A wise, witty, and often wicked voice." —*USA Today*

"Rouse is a master raconteur and his transition from city slicker to country mouse is filled with sidesplitting humor, heart, and, of course, bands of marauding raccoons. This book has now taken its place at the top of my favorites list!" —Jen Lancaster

"A funny, good-natured chronicle of a fish out of water, slowly learning to breathe."
—Tom Perrotta, *New York Times* bestselling author of
The Abstinence Teacher

"In the spirit of David Sedaris, a laugh-out-loud funny book!"
—John Searles on NBC's *Today* show

"You laugh when you least expect to—and then you realize you've been laughing almost nonstop." —*Detroit Free Press*

"This is David Sedaris meets Dave Berry. . . . Every page is good for a laugh." —*Library Journal*

"Immensely entertaining."
—A. J. Jacobs, *New York Times* bestselling author of
The Year of Living Biblically

I'm Not the Biggest Bitch in This Relationship

HILARIOUS, HEARTWARMING TALES
ABOUT MAN'S BEST FRIEND
FROM AMERICA'S FAVORITE HUMORISTS

EDITED BY WADE ROUSE

Foreword by Chelsea Handler's Dog, Chunk

 NEW AMERICAN LIBRARY

NEW AMERICAN LIBRARY
Published by New American Library, a division of
Penguin Group (USA) Inc., 375 Hudson Street,
New York, New York 10014, USA
Penguin Group (Canada), 90 Eglinton Avenue East, Suite 700, Toronto,
Ontario M4P 2Y3, Canada (a division of Pearson Penguin Canada Inc.)
Penguin Books Ltd., 80 Strand, London WC2R 0RL, England
Penguin Ireland, 25 St. Stephen's Green, Dublin 2,
Ireland (a division of Penguin Books Ltd.)
Penguin Group (Australia), 250 Camberwell Road, Camberwell, Victoria 3124,
Australia (a division of Pearson Australia Group Pty. Ltd.)
Penguin Books India Pvt. Ltd., 11 Community Centre, Panchsheel Park,
New Delhi - 110 017, India
Penguin Group (NZ), 67 Apollo Drive, Rosedale, Auckland 0632,
New Zealand (a division of Pearson New Zealand Ltd.)
Penguin Books (South Africa) (Pty.) Ltd., 24 Sturdee Avenue,
Rosebank, Johannesburg 2196, South Africa

Penguin Books Ltd., Registered Offices:
80 Strand, London WC2R 0RL, England

First published by New American Library,
a division of Penguin Group (USA) Inc.

First Printing, September 2011
10   9   8   7   6   5   4   3   2   1

 REGISTERED TRADEMARK—MARCA REGISTRADA

LIBRARY OF CONGRESS CATALOGING-IN-PUBLICATION DATA:

I'm not the biggest bitch in this relationship: hilarious, heartwarming tales about man's best friends from America's favorite humorists/edited by Wade Rouse; foreword by Chelsea Handler's dog, Chunk.
    p. cm.
    ISBN 978-0-451-23458-2
    1. Dogs—United States—Anecdotes. 2. Dogs—Humor. 3. Humorists, American—Biography—Anecdotes. I. Rouse, Wade.
    SF426.2.I5 2011
    636.7—dc23   2011020250

Set in Berkley
Designed by Patrice Sheridan

Printed in the United States of America

For Marge
July 16, 1997–April 11, 2011

Fourteen years, five books, three major life changes, thousands of
walks, millions of kisses, billions of silent farts, zillions of snuggles,
infinite belly rubs, laughs and treats…

and one man whose life has forever been changed by one rescue
dog's unconditional love. You helped teach me it was OK to love
again, with wild abandon, heart be damned.

For Mabel

You make me laugh. You remind me to play like a child. You sleep on
my legs until they are numb. You wake me at dawn to start the day.
You were your sister's keeper.

Contents

Contents

I'm Not the Biggest Bitch in This Relationship

My Best Paw Foreword

Chelsea Handler's Dog, Chunk

Hello. My name is Chunk Handler.

I'm a chow mixed with a handsome dash of German shepherd. I'm a dog. A canine. A mutt. A fleabag. I have four furry legs and a missing pair of nuts, and I refer to most girls as bitches. I dream in color, but my life is in black and white.

Let's go on a walk—careful though, I tend to pull the leash. Don't forget a plastic baggie, because I tend to take big dumps. My mom is Chelsea Handler. She's a comedian, a television host, and a bestselling author. If you don't know who she is, don't worry. When I met her I had no idea who she was, either. That's probably because I don't watch the E! channel. I mainly enjoy classic film noir, but I also like any dating show that involves a slut bus.

When I was approached to contribute to this book, I was naturally annoyed. I mean what . . . a pain in the ass. Typically, the only thing I like to do with an ass is sniff it. The idea of writing a foreword for a book about a bunch of idiots and their mutts sounded awful, but it did get me thinking about where I came from. I'm a long walk away from where I was about a year ago.

Once upon a time, I was just some poor shelter pooch with an expiration date. I was like a carton of spoiling milk.

Just one year ago . . .

It was springtime in Los Angeles; the irony that everything else was in bloom all around me while I was in my dire situation wasn't lost on me. I was stuck at the West Los Angeles Animal Shelter, and it was the day I was sentenced to be assassinated. They were going to electrocute me in a cute little doggy electric chair. Everything that's little and doggy usually sounds so adorable, but an electric chair sounds sick. I don't believe that's how they were actually going to kill me. It's just a little gallows humor.

So, humor me.

I thought I'd get shot by a firing squad or something.

Here's a rule of non-opposable thumb: If you ever end up in a place with the word "shelter" in it, life's not going great for you. Like a bomb shelter. That's pretty bad. Or, if you're sheltered as a kid, and when you grow up you can't relate to the adult world. It's like how most men expect to have sex on the first date. You're kind of screwed there, too.

Most dogs don't care much about dying. We don't sit around fearing the end on a daily basis like humans do. You never see a dog with a cardboard sign hanging around his neck that says "The End Is Near." The only end I want near . . . is a rear end. But when it's actually happening to you, I don't care if you're a dog or a bumblebee or a little cell inside a dumb fish, you won't want to die. Trust me, girl.

The biggest regret about my life is that I never felt like I was a part of anything. I always felt more like I was apart from everything. It's funny how "a part" and "apart" are complete opposites, yet only differ by a little space.

God, I'm deep.

My entire life I'd been passed around from one family to the next more times than the common cold. I've gone by a dozen different names, from Cinnamon to Escalade. It was a black family that named me Escalade. What a shocker. Nothing against black people, they just come up with really stupid names. I mean, white people are crazy, too. This one hick from Texas named me Booger. He would always try to feed me his boogers. What an a-hole. Right now, my name is Guinness. I hate that name, it sounds so pedestrian for a dog of my taste.

On the other paw, I guess it doesn't really matter what my name is. A name is just a sound that someone utters to get someone else to turn around. You could call me Litter Box Dump and I'd be fine with that. So, go off.

I suppose what this all adds up to is that I've never been a good enough dog to capture the heart of just one person who could love me forever. It's probably my fault.

In fact, somehow I've earned the reputation in the shelter world as being a "problem dog." Please don't ever give a dog a reputation. It's a loser thing to do. We're just who we are.

We bark, we bite, we chew, and we shadoobie. So, get used to it.

I don't really want to die, but it's not like I want to sit around the shelter and watch Cesar Millan on National Geographic for the rest of my life, either. I'm just a tail wagger on the red list, and there's only two ways off the red list. I either go home in a loving person's car or in a doggy bag. At least all dogs go to heaven, right?

And that's where my life got weird.

See, that should have been my last thought. All dogs go to heaven. I'd been rehearsing it for years. I should've been shot to sleep. Everything should've faded to black. The end.

But it wasn't.

There are a thousand dogs, in a thousand shelters, on a thousand different days. I don't know why she did, but she walked into mine. I felt like Humphrey Bogart in *Casablanca*, and Chelsea was my sweet Ingrid Bergman. She was like a vision in faux blond strutting into that shelter, and she rescued me.

The first thing I did when I met Chelsea . . . I smelled her coslopus.

You can learn so much from smelling someone's crotch. Why do you think dogs always smell each other's assholes? It's instant knowledge. It's like everything that encompasses that person is downloaded right into your brain the instant you take a whiff.

Chelsea's coslopus smelled like a mystery. As I climbed into the back of her Jaguar, I didn't know where I was going or what was in store for my future. But I did think the backseat was a little tight. I didn't give two craps about it, though. I was just happy to be alive. I stuck my head out the window and let the salty Santa Monica air blow through my coat, and I screamed at the top of my lungs.

"Woof!"

Now, just getting rescued is one thing. But getting rescued by a celebrity is like winning the lottery powerball scratcher mega millions jackpot bingo hole in one.

I went from the red list to the B-list in one day.

Well, maybe not the B-list, but at least the C-plus-list.

This type of rags-to-riches life has to happen to somebody, though. It made me feel like one of Brad and Angelina's adopted kids. Imagine that sense of surreal luck. You're living in Cambodia, and then one day Angelina Jolie swoops in and rescues you. It almost seems more miraculous than actually being one of their genetic offspring.

I'm like Chelsea's Maddox.

Thank God, she hated the name Guinness. And since Maddox was already taken, Chelsea looked at me and said, "I'm going to call you Chunk."

As much as I love the sound of that, I try not getting too attached to my names. I mean, there's always that chance it won't last. I've had it happen a million times. I'm sitting at a shelter, and a little girl pleads, "Oh, Daddy, please can I have a puppy?! Pleeaaase can I have him?!"

The daddy begrudgingly agrees, but only after making his young daughter promise to take the dog on walks, and pick up the shadoobs, and do all the other hard work that goes along with having a dog.

Notice how I didn't say "owning" a dog. You don't "own" a dog. You "have" a dog. And the dog has you.

The problem is that one day that little girl gets bored with the dog, and she yearns for boys, and then she forgets about the dog. Shortly after that, her daddy gets tired of taking the dog on walks, and tired of feeding the dog, and that's how the dog ends up back in the shelter. I just don't want my relationship with Chelsea to end like that.

I remember seeing this old cartoon when I was a puppy. There are these two polar bears standing next to an igloo. One of the polar bears has just taken a bite out of the igloo, and he says:

"I love these things, they're crunchy on the outside, and chewy in the center."

That's how I feel: a little icy on the outside, but soft at heart.

For a while after Chelsea took me home, I had a pretty bad case of the separation anxieties. To be honest, I've never been able to leave Chelsea's side. When she goes to the bathroom, I sit by the door. That goes for number ones and number twos. She once said that she'd never let a dog sleep in her bed. Well, guess where I sleep? I sleep in her bed. Sometimes I fart, and we laugh. I wag my tail to waft the stench around the room. Don't always assume that if a dog is wagging his tail that means he's happy to see you. A lot of times it just means he farted, or that he's giving you the finger.

If you're a fan of Chelsea's idiot-box television show called *Chelsea Lately*, then you've probably seen me wandering around the set from time to time. I'm practically quasi-famous. If only the mutts at the shelter could see me now. Soon, Chelsea and I will be moving into a big house, with a big backyard, and a big pool. I'd invite all the old dogs over if I knew where they were.

I can't believe it was just a year ago that I was supposed to be electrocuted in a little doggy electric chair. These days, I fly around the globe on private jets; I spend weekends with Chelsea's hot friend Jenny McCarthy. I even have my own Twitter page to vent my frustrations. You can follow me at @chunkhandler, by the way.

I mean, I'm living the life.

That got me thinking about this book, and why it was important that I contributed. All these people came together to write about how much they love their stupid mutts. Well, I think one mutt had to come forward and say how much we love you guys, too. We aren't very picky, either. You don't have to be a celebrity to win us over. Most of the time all we need is someone who talks to us, rubs our belly, and picks our poops off the ground. I realize that we're the dogs and you're the humans, and you literally rescued us. But remember that we all play our own part.

We all save each other.

Chelsea always said that she didn't want to be a mother. But whether she likes it or not, now she is a mother. She has a son, and my name is Chunk. And I finally feel like I'm not apart from everything, but I am a part of something greater than myself.

My name isn't just a sound that someone utters to get me to turn around anymore. My name is Chunk.

I am Chunk.

Now pardon me while I drop a shadoobie.

Dum-Diddle-Dum-Dum

Wade Rouse

"Sit! *Sit!*" the trainer screamed at me the second Saturday of puppy obedience class.

Since the six-foot-four woman made Xena the Warrior Princess look like Kate Moss and had the voice and decibel level of a cement mixer, I promptly took a seat on the floor next to twenty other puppies.

"*No!* Not you! Your dog!" she bellowed, nodding her Amazon-sized head at our puppy, Marge, who was now sitting on my lap. "She isn't listening! You should have her hearing tested."

I stood, handed my partner, Gary, the dog and the leash, and walked over to stand in Xena's shade. I motioned for her to lean down, and whispered into her elephant ear, "Her hearing is fine. *You're* not speaking her language."

"Excuse me!" she yelled, so loudly, in fact, that her perfectly trained German shepherd, Hans—who, to this point, I had begun to believe was operated via remote control because he *never* moved without instruction—lifted his ears. "That'll be enough, Hans!" she yelled at the dog, who immediately bowed at her boots.

"You're not speaking Marge's language," I whispered again, attempting to sound as rational as I could. "Or using the right voice."

"What, exactly, is Marge's language? And voice?"

It was here that the Halti-dispensing behemoth smirked in my face, copping the same expression and tone that Eileen Brennan used in *Private Benjamin* the first time she saw Goldie Hawn in the army.

"Go on! Tell the class!" she said and motioned with her tree limb.

I turned to face roughly twenty other dog owners, all sucking down lattes in North Face jackets, and their puppies, outfitted in bright bandanas and expensive collars.

"Well, it's sort of a special lexicon that we've taught Marge." I smiled creepily, as if I were standing in front of the judges in my Wow Wear performing my "Sassy Walk." I smiled prettily, hoping these well-bred, by-the-book owners and pets might just suddenly forget what was happening.

"Go on!" barked the trainer.

And then, for the first time, just like she had hoped, I realized I had to explain this insanity to the world, retract the curtain and let everyone see that the wizard was actually Joaquin Phoenix, a mass of quirks and instability.

"Enlighten us!" Xena growled again, a mortified Hans seeming to smile at someone else's predicament.

So, I raised my voice roughly four octaves, and said as rationally as I could in my Alvin and the Chipmunks falsetto, "Margie! Itty-bitty-boo!"

The yuppie crowd doubled over in laughter, and applauded, like they were watching a seal perch a striped beach ball on its nose. But, above the din, our mutt, Marge—our little rescue Heinz 57, who fit in with these purebreds as much as me and Gary—did as instructed: She sat on my command.

"'Itty-bitty-boo' means 'sit'?" the trainer bellowed.

"Yes!" I said in my falsetto, before correcting myself. "Yes!"

"And how, pray tell, would you say 'Come!'?" Xena asked.

"Dum-diddle-dum-dum, Margie!" I chimed.

And our reddish puppy—her giant paws still too big for her burgeoning frame—rushed over to me, dragging her leash.

It was then that the crowd took on a different emotion, a mix of enchantment and disbelief, like fanatics do when they discover the image of Jesus in a Pringle.

"Enough!" the trainer yelled. "You have spoiled your dog. She will learn the commands as taught—*the normal way*—like the rest of us. Everyone here speaks the same language. Marge, sit!"

Marge looked up at the trainer and barked.

"Marge, sit!"

Marge looked over at me and barked.

"Marge, sit!"

And, with that, Xena walked over, bent to the floor, and forced Marge to the ground, yelling, "Sit! Marge, sit!"

Marge battled her every inch of the way, finally succumbing with a sad yelp.

"She only understands simple, direct commands in a forceful tone," the trainer barked at me. "Have a backbone. You must be the leader of the pack. She doesn't understand you. Say a simple, direct command in a forceful tone."

"You're a Nazi bitch!" Gary suddenly said.

Cue crickets: Everyone stopped breathing, even the energetic puppies.

That command, it seemed, everyone understood.

"Let's go, Wade," Gary yelled. "Marge! Dum-diddle-dum-dum!"

And, with that, our wacky little family left class.

On the drive home, as I nuzzled my mutt with the soulful brown eyes, thick auburn fur, a white stripe going up her nose like a highway divider, and the fuzziest ears I'd ever felt, I seriously wondered if we had jacked her up right out of the gate, if she would be a rotten baby, churlish teenager, spoiled, selfish adult.

Gary caught the look on my face, and said, "No one there spoke our language, Wade," before inserting a CD of the musical *Chicago*, which he knew would make me smile. As we sang the lyrics to "All That Jazz"—"I'm gonna rouge my knees/And roll my stockings down"—*Bam! Bam!*—I began to think of the opening scene in *Terms of Endearment*, where a baby Debra Winger is sleeping soundly, and momma Shirley MacLaine isn't satisfied that her newborn daughter is okay until she pinches her, and the baby starts howling.

In essence, that's how our dysfunction started.

Gary and I adopted Marge from a city shelter because, as a happy new couple, we wanted a family. Marge was from a litter of fourteen, which was unceremoniously dumped in a large box in an alley. We were fed a bunch of lies about her—told she would grow to be only fifty pounds, whereas she topped out at nearly eighty-five; told she was a prime candidate for potty training since she always peed on the newspaper, though she would battle a leaky bladder for life—but we picked her largely because, out of the hundreds of abandoned dogs at the shelter, she immediately responded to our voices.

Our falsetto voices, to be accurate.

Gary and I often create characters—much like *Saturday Night Live* cast members do—to skewer the world around us. We did so that day at the shelter, after touring the facility with a hard-edged urban professional in a power suit, a redneck couple whose wife was so hungover she kept pulling her Busch beer bandana over her eyes to "squeeze out the damn light," and a bosomy woman in a glitter tube top with a tattoo across her chest that read, "Big Enuf 4 Ya?" who was in the market for a dog to provide "a little protection."

Thus, that day, Gary and I created Ne-ne (the successful, professional city woman), Connie (the hard-luck, hard-partying gal who couldn't hold a job), and Trixie (the town whore).

Standing in front of Marge and her brood, it was quite a while before we unconsciously began doing our characters, each of whom was defined by an oddly high-pitched voice and caustic, snarky, biting wit, almost as if Sarah Silverman had just ingested a helium-filled balloon.

Marge immediately took notice. And so did we.

"Mr. Tutwiler," Gary said to Marge, as if he were Connie, "git'cher hands off the forklift and back on my ass where they belong!"

"Twenty bucks? Twenty bucks!" I screamed à la Trixie, licking cake-batter-flavored gloss off my lips. "That won't even get you a flash of my teats and a date to Taco Bell!"

"My God!" Gary screamed, as the tiny puppy scrambled up our chests and into our arms to kiss our faces, while the others hid. "She loves it! She speaks our language!"

It was a sign, because very few in either of our lives had, really.

My older brother, Todd, died when I was thirteen, and though he was the exact opposite of me—a true country boy who loved to fish and hunt and work on motorcycles—we had a special relationship, and often communicated via a secret language.

"If you ever get into trouble and I'm nearby," Todd would tell me, "yell 'Suzuki!' [his favorite motorcycle], and I'll be right there."

And I did. Many times. And he was always there to protect me.

Gary lost every man he loved, in quick succession, all of whom used their words as weapons to wound Gary's heart, kill his faith in the power of love, murder his innocence and optimism until he was no longer needed, and he was left abandoned, empty, alone, unable to speak.

Yes—though Marge was just a puppy who couldn't even speak—it seemed nearly miraculous for both of us to stumble upon such an obvious, uplifting sign: Marge symbolized our language of love.

We immediately attempted to crate train Marge as a puppy—as the shelter, vet, and all our friends instructed—but her sad howling from the family room kept us awake for endless nights, until, finally, blessedly, there was silence.

But we verbal addicts mistook that sign of success as imminent death, much like Shirley MacLaine, and so Gary and I took turns sleeping on a blanketed air mattress outside her crate, to ensure that our puppy was, indeed, alive. We crammed cramped fingers through the openings in the gate so we could feel the air coming from her nose. We shook her awake when she seemed to be too quiet. We smiled when she would howl and then immediately quiet upon hearing our Daffy Duck–meets–Kathy Griffin impressions.

Only when I could no longer use my keyboard at work without flinching in pain and Gary could no longer blow-dry his hair did we remove our fingers and move Marge from crate to our bed, where we cooed and sang, and, slowly, began to create an even bigger cast of characters to entertain Marge—and one another—each of whom used a virtual pre-*Avatar* language, a bizarre lexicon understood by only the three of us.

Soon, it became the only language to which Marge would respond.

I began compiling this language, and its many terms, which we termed "Marge-ese":

Potty-pee = Go tinkle!
Potty-poo = Go poop!
Bites = Food
Nink-nink = Water or Drink your water
Git-um-good-ums = Eat your food
Seepy weepy = Time for bed
Wuboo! = I love you
Stinky-winky-woo = Time for a bath!

In addition to Ne-ne, Connie, and Trixie, we added Maria (which was Marge's given name, a sassy, sexy, but bitter Penélope Cruz understudy); Sasha (a proud but poor Russian woman forced to beg for bread); Anastasia (a rich European who only shopped in Prague, but secretly loved to down Sliders at White Castle); and Ms. Betty Lou Tuttlesworth (a bedraggled secretary who could never speak up for herself and whose boss used to always drop his pencil for her to stoop over and pick up).

Over time, our Marge-ese dictionary and cast list were given to friends and relatives as well as our vet, so they could communicate with our dog, understand her. But no one really took us seriously. That is, until Gary and I went on our first vacation since adopting Marge, and we gave our dictionary to the kennel where Marge was staying.

Three days into our stay in Puerto Vallarta, we received a call saying Marge had yet to eat, drink, or even sleep since we had left.

"Are you speaking her language?" we asked. "Or doing a character?"

"Ummm, we tried," the owner said, more than just a hint of malice in her voice. "We've tried to get her to play with other dogs, but she doesn't seem interested. And we've tried hamburger and rice, and special biscuits. She's not responding to anything. Except cartoons on TV. She's just looking around for you."

"Put us on speaker," Gary said.

And, in the high-pitched, cartoon voices only she could understand, we told her to eat, drink, and potty. Which continued the next four days.

I thought of Xena, our puppy trainer, while trying—but failing—to relax in Mexico. She was right. We had created a nightmare. One, now, that would never end.

From that point on, Gary and I really never left Marge. Whenever we traveled—vacation, book tour, holiday—Marge was there, riding in between us. And if she couldn't go, Gary's parents—who were nearly as neurotic as we were—babysat, following our dictionary, word for word, performing characters left and right, as if they were doing improv on a Japanese game show.

Marge eventually—as dogs do—leapfrogged us in years. She is now thirteen.

She has seen us through our early thirties into our mid-forties.

She has developed gray hair alongside us. She gets stiff after exercising. And, for nearly a decade and a half, this eighty-plus-pound mutt has lain—day in and day out—on my feet, as I wrote and tried to make sense of the world via words, my own language.

After four books, Marge is still the first person to hear what I write—yes, I read to her in falsetto—and she listens more intensely than any other reader or fan I've ever known.

Marge has helped shepherd me and Gary through a sea change of triumphs and traumas: a move to the woods of Michigan, a career as a full-time writer, along with the loss of my mother to cancer, and the loss of Gary's grandmother. But I feel more capable of handling life now, thanks to her. Though I realize that life on this planet is but a blink of an eye, and that time is not the vast ocean I once believed it was—endless and infinite—but more like a creek, a quick swim from one shore to the other, Marge has taught me to appreciate the beauty of each day, to not think about time or the future, only to sigh, and kiss and play, and love and laugh without limit.

Still, whenever I begin to become a turtle again, Marge coaxes me to get up and walk with her and talk to her. She forces me to pause and look up at the sky with her, to chase seagulls on the beach with her, to swim in icy Lake Michigan with her—our dueling, dog-paddling shadows on the sandy surface below giving me hope that everyone can find that special someone with whom to swim through life. She, like Gary, has retaught me that it is okay to love, no matter the risk.

Recently, one evening, after eating her dinner, after a day of playing in the snow and chomping at snowballs, Marge could not seem to get comfortable. She followed me and Gary around so closely that her nose became part of our thighs.

I bent down and looked Marge directly in her big brown doe eyes.

She let out a sad, mournful yelp, put a paw on my chest, and then dry-heaved three times. I felt her nose. It was ice cold.

"Call the vet!" I yelled à la Alvin.

Twenty minutes later we were at the vet's office. Diagnosis? A turned stomach, just like in *Marley and Me*. Prognosis? Fifty-fifty chance of survival, less considering her age.

As the needle slid into Marge's furry arm, and the vet scooted Marge away on a gurney, Gary and I looked at her and said, "Wuboo! Seepy weepy!"

Her tail lazily thumped the stainless steel a few times and then she was off, but not before I could grab the gurney—just as her eyes began to glaze over—and tell my mutt, in a bizarre falsetto and the only words I could muster, "You cannot leave me, do you understand? It is not time. I need you!"

Marge gave me one last kiss.

The vet called at three a.m., after four hours of surgery, and said, miraculously, that Marge had made it through. But the worst was not yet over. She had been open for a long time, and was now under heat lamps to warm her body temperature. Three hours later, the vet called again. Marge was awake, alert, and looking for us.

"I've never seen owners get a dog with a turned stomach into the vet more quickly. You saved her life. You really do speak the same language," the vet said. "She's looking for you. Better come take her home."

We picked Marge up—who was cut from here to kingdom come—and Gary said, in Marge's helium-filled vibrato, "I got the tummy tuck you boys will never afford!"

Day by day, as Marge recovered, we found ourselves in the

same position as we had when she was a puppy. Lying on the floor, holding her, speaking bizarre words in a high pitch only the three of us could understand. When Marge would wake and hear us, or catch us staring at her, her eyes would immediately widen, brighten, and her tail would give off a pathetic but telling thump, thump, thump. I don't know how much time I have left with her, but Marge has taught me to cherish each day, each kiss, each falsetto word, rather than fear the final outcome.

Marge has trained me, you see, to be a stronger person.

Ironically, I happened to see Xena, Marge's puppy trainer, not long after Marge's miracle recovery, while doing a book event in our former city. She was in the big dog park, training two German shepherds, and I was talking to Marge as if she were Ne-ne and missed her days as a big-city career gal.

My falsetto must have been the key that unlocked some past trauma for Xena, for she approached me, after thirteen years, and said, "It is Marge, right?"

I nodded.

"And did she ever learn to sit properly?" she asked.

"It depends on what you mean by 'properly,' " I said. "Itty-bitty-boo."

And Marge sat.

"That's just . . . well . . . amazing," she said, looking at Marge as if she were an idiot savant. "Amazing she was able to learn so much."

"No, what's amazing is how much I was able to learn."

Her face took on that bemused Eileen Brennan expression again, and I asked, "When did you lose Hans?"

"How could you tell? Everyone thinks my dogs all look the same."

"Hans used to smile," I said.

"Itty-bitty-boo," Xena said, out of the blue, her expression suddenly bright. And Marge sat.

"That's just amazing," she said once again.

Marge and I took off running through the grass, in the brilliant sunshine, me chatting to her in our bizarre lexicon. Finally, I took a seat in the shade of a giant oak, and my best friend put her paws in my lap and gave me a kiss. I cradled Marge's giant old head in my hands—because that's how we roll—and the two of us chatted about this strange world, this world of strays, of mutts and men, all of whom have to overcome great odds to find that perfect someone who loves us unconditionally, who embraces our quirks and neuroses, that special someone who, quite simply, speaks our language.

A Dog Day
of Summer

W. Bruce Cameron

Dear Dog,

This is what happened.

You woke up this morning at seven a.m. It being a Saturday, I was still asleep. You became concerned that I might be getting too much rest, so you came over and shoved your wet nose in my face.

When I rolled over with a groan, you realized your intentions had been misunderstood. You watched me lie there, my breathing slowing, for a full minute before you barked in frustration.

"No barking," I muttered. "Lie down. Sleep."

You sifted carefully through this statement, completely comprehending that I had not used the word "bacon." You barked again, and then again.

I rolled over and looked at you. "What? What is it?" I asked you.

You wagged excitedly. *Yes!* you thought. *Let's get up!* Now your barking and yipping took on a frantic note. *Time to get up! Time to get up!*

"Okay, okay!" I said. I got out of bed and got dressed. You

watched attentively. I went into the kitchen and started the coffee. You raced over to your favorite spot in front of the fireplace, stretched out on your dog bed, and *fell asleep.* I suppose you thought that as long as one of us was awake, the house was secure and the other member of the team should use the opportunity to catch up on some badly needed rest.

Me. *I* needed the rest. But you were the one who slept.

You roused yourself, of course, when I brought breakfast to the table. You sat alertly and obediently at my side, watching every spoonful of oatmeal as I raised it to my lips. My attention was riveted by the newspaper because I have several excellent ideas for fixing all the world's problems and want to be prepared for when the president telephones. You put a paw on my leg.

I looked down at you and realized you had not been informed of recent developments concerning my bloodstream and the amount of cholesterol that's floating around in it like an oil slick. "It's oatmeal," I said to you.

You swallowed, nearly swooning with food lust.

"You wouldn't like it. Get your paw off my leg. No. I will not feed you."

You heard a firmness in my tone and dropped your eyes in a wounded fashion. *Okay, I guess I'll just die of starvation, but I'm willing if it will make you happy,* your expression said. You fell to the floor dramatically, your face a study in tragedy. You took a long, shuddering sigh, then glanced up at me to see if I was buying it. I was back to reading about world events.

Well, this was intolerable. You jumped to your feet and walked over to your empty food bowl, which you pointedly licked, your dog tags clanging against the metal rim. Your whole life, the rule is you don't get to eat until I do, but that doesn't prevent you from staging your regularly scheduled protest demonstration each and every morning.

I ate as much oatmeal as I could swallow, which wasn't much. The doctor says replacing bacon and eggs with this stuff will help me live longer. My response: Why would I want to?

When I stood up from the table, you began doing your dance, a dervish's whirl, whipping yourself around in circles while still keeping your eyes on my face. I don't understand why your head doesn't twist off when you do this.

"There is no bacon," I warned you. "You really don't want my leftovers."

You nearly passed out at the word "bacon." You were panting and trembling and drooling as I picked up your bowl and put in dog food. I turned to look at you and you froze, your gaze intent.

"You really want oatmeal?"

Yes! You danced some more. *Yes! Yes! Yes!*

I shrugged and shoveled some of the vile stuff into your bowl. Maybe you'll live longer, too.

I put the bowl on the floor and you lunged for it, inhaling your meal, choking your food down as if I were about to take it away from you in mid-meal, which just for the record I have never, ever done. And then you froze. You pulled your head back a little, sniffing. Then you turned and stared at me.

Hey, your look said, *what the hell is this?*

"I told you. It's oatmeal."

You went back to eating, but now, instead of great gulps, you ate daintily, chewing with just the front teeth, as if you were trying to skin a tomato. With every swallow you shot me a searing, accusatory glance.

When you were finished I peered into your bowl: A slimy pile of oatmeal lay at the bottom. You watched grumpily as I cleaned it out.

Normally when I go back to brush my teeth and get ready to face the day you follow me and tangle yourself in my legs, but normally there'd been a tiny piece of bacon for you in your breakfast bowl. Without the bacon, life just seemed to have lost its purpose. This particular morning you went back to lie in front of the fireplace, sighing mournfully.

You didn't rouse yourself until the next-door neighbor went out into his backyard, and then you hurled yourself against the back window, barking ferociously.

"Hey," I said, "cut it out. You know Mr. Morton, you like Mr. Morton. It's his yard, for heaven's sake."

You wouldn't listen to my treasonous suggestion that we leave the invader alone. Then Mr. Morton started trimming his hedges, which so offended you that you nearly strangled on your own barking. You banged your face against the window, drooling and snapping your teeth.

"Okay! Okay!" I shouted. I went to the front door and opened it and you pushed me out of the way, your face set in a lethal snarl, your legs scrabbling for purchase. You rocketed out into the yard, a dog on a mission of death, straight for Mr. Morton, who looked up at your murderous approach.

Then you seemed to have second thoughts. Maybe I was right, maybe Mr. Morton was a nice guy. Maybe he should be allowed to trim his own hedges in his own yard without being killed by a dog attack. And hey, wasn't there something interesting to sniff at the bottom of this one tree, here? Can't we all get along?

Mr. Morton patted his thighs and you went over to him, wagging your tail, and then flopped over for a belly rub. I watched your complete submission with an ironic expression that was completely lost on you when you came bouncing back into the yard. *It's Mr. Morton!* your expression said. *We love him!*

"Okay, come on in," I said, holding the door open.

You started to obey, and then you stopped, a thought flitting into your brain with such clarity I could actually see it register. It was a beautiful July day. I was probably going to sit at the computer all day long. There were scents to follow and bushes to mark, and, most important of all, there had been no bacon.

Your ears flattened themselves on either side of your head, a sure sign that you were thinking of being a bad dog. You glanced down the road, toward freedom.

"Come here," I said sternly.

We've practiced this command over and over—when I use that tone of voice, you know from experience that I am asserting my alpha authority over you, and that also, if you do as you are told, I will give you a treat. The powerful combination of dominance and reward are as compelling to you as a T-bone; it's as if I'd turned on my *Star Trek* tractor beam and was pulling you with inexorable force back into the house.

You took off.

"Come! Stay! Heel!" I shouted. These are all words in your limited vocabulary, and they all mean you are supposed to do what I say, so you increased your speed, until you were galloping like a greyhound after a rabbit.

You know that you are superior to me, physically. I may be able to throw a Frisbee, but you can chew one up. I can hurl a tennis ball down the street, but you can catch it in midair and then soak it in saliva so that I won't want to touch it. And you can run faster. I will never catch you.

Your favorite playmate in the world is a black Labrador named Napoleon. Once you felt you had traveled far enough that I would never be able to find you, you veered through some backyards over to Napoleon's kennel. He greeted you joyously through the fence, and his owner went out to let you in to wrestle with your playmate.

Caller ID told me who was phoning me. I picked up the phone. "I know," I said.

My neighbor told me you were welcome to stay as long as you wanted. I sighed and said that no, I felt that would only reinforce the behavior. I got in my car and drove over there.

You looked up, startled, when my car's familiar sounds told you I had arrived in Napoleon's driveway. Despite the fact that every single time you have ever run away you have gone straight to Napoleon's house, you are dumbfounded that I have tracked you down.

I got out of my car and stood with my hands on my hips, which is the posture I adopt whenever you get into the garbage or chew one of my shoes or do anything that I know you know is bad. You lowered your head. Napoleon used the distraction to jump on you and put his mouth on your neck. You whirled and put your mouth on *his* neck. The wrestling recommenced.

"Hey!" I called out sternly.

You regarded me, puzzled, not sure why I sounded so mad. Then you remembered, and you dropped your head again. *Oh, yeah, the running-away thing.*

I let you out of the kennel, pushing Napoleon's eager head back so he didn't get out, too. You were slinking now, your belly close to the ground. "You were a bad dog," I told you.

Yes, a very, very bad dog. So bad, your expression said as I led you to the car. I opened the passenger door and you slipped inside, hanging your head. *A bad, bad dog.*

I went around and got in my side. You greeted me as if you'd been locked in the car for an hour, licking me and wagging your tail so hard it sent ripples of energy up and down your whole body. *Car ride?* your expression said. *We going for a car ride?*

I spoke sternly to you, delivering my lecture on Expected Dog Behavior, but it was such a grand day you were too happy to pay much attention. You stuck your nose into the wind through the open window, took in several deep sniffs, then brought your head inside and sprayed me with a wet sneeze.

"Yuck!" I said.

We pulled in our driveway and you spotted Mr. Morton and began barking ferociously. *Let me at him, I'll kill the bastard!*

"Stop it," I told you. I clicked the leash onto your collar and you gave me a wounded look. *What's that for?*

You continued to growl and bark at Mr. Morton while I went around to let you out. I snagged the end of the leash and you strained against it, begging for an opportunity to attack our neighbor. He waved at me, and I waved back.

Struggling, I pulled you back into the house and shut the door. I removed the leash and you went to the window, still snarling, as Mr. Morton put away his hedge clippers and disappeared through his back door. The fur was up on your back, but you gradually began to stand down from full alert. You'd scared the guy back into his house, thus saving all of us from his mad hedge clipping. You had protected our property.

"Okay," I said. "You are not supposed to run away, do you understand me? You come when I call."

You responded to the one word you recognized, "come," by

trotting obediently over to me and sitting alertly at my feet. *See what a good dog I am? Want me to heel? Stay? You name it.*

"I have to work on a column. We'll go for a walk this afternoon, okay?"

Walk? You liked the sound of that, but then you groaned when I went over to the computer and sat down at the keyboard. *Not again!*

I began to peck away. You sniffed around a little, and then an inspiration hit you and you went to your food bowl. You dipped your face into it, inhaling deeply. Then you raised your head and gave me a look of pure, stunned disbelief

What? your eyes seemed to say. *No bacon?*

I looked away, concentrating on my column. It was due the day before, which meant I really needed to finish it in the next day or two. My editor and I have an agreement that it's not really, *really* late until it is three days late, so I try to adhere to a strict schedule of only being two days late, though usually I'm four days late.

You came over and put your head in my lap. I looked down at your sad eyes and realized that I had never been so hungry—whatever they put in oatmeal, apparently they leave out *food*. You whimpered.

You're starving, you seemed to be saying to me. *I don't want you to starve.*

You're my best friend in the world—if you were worried about me, didn't that mean something?

I made BLTs for lunch, reasoning the doctor had only warned me about bacon for breakfast. You were really happy when I slipped a piece of it to you under the table.

And I was happy, too.

Dogs Are the
New Children

Jen Lancaster

We were never going to be the kind of people who had kids.

Instead, we were going to be the kind of people who had *dogs*.

From the onset of our relationship, my then boyfriend, now husband, Fletcher, and I had strong feelings on the concept of child rearing. Said feelings could be neatly summed up in exactly one word—no.

To be clear, it's not as though we hated children or denied their right to exist. Rather, we likened having kids to piercing one's lip or commissioning an elaborate neck tattoo—painful, permanent, and a poor use of disposable income.*

My husband was concerned that as two smug, self-satisfied Yuppies, we were too selfish to have kids, that we prized our orderly home, the ability to sleep late, and the overall feeling of peace and quiet far too much to ever want to reproduce. He worried that the combination of our naturally controlling and contrarian DNA would spawn some kind of serial killer–supervillain, or

*But, like, okay for some people. Just not us.

at the very least, the kind of kid who'd milk us for four years of undergrad followed by an Ivy League law school, only to then graduate and decide his/her true calling was the Peace Corps.

For me, I was perfectly okay with children . . . in a limited context. I mean, I could appreciate seeing little faces wreathed in smiles on a swing set or heading into a Pixar film. I practically felt their joy when they lined up next to the ice cream truck or gazed into the seal tank at the zoo, their wee snub noses pressed up against the glass. Kids could be cute. That is, as long as they went home with someone else.

Also? In terms of the physical effort having a child would involve, I didn't particularly like carrying anything heavier than my purse, and that whole watermelon-through-a-keyhole business? Again, *no*.

My husband and I were on board with the concept of opening our home and sharing our lives—just not with any creature that had the ability to borrow our cars without asking, get their prom date pregnant, or permanently etch their love for said prom date on their neck. We were never going to parent anything we couldn't actively control, meaning we'd never be those assholes in the restaurant who'd simply smile and shrug their shoulders as their progeny colored on the walls and ground Goldfish crackers into the floor. *We* believed in discipline. *We* were the ones running the show. And since tolerating nothing but utter and complete obedience sounded more than a little *Mommie Dearest*, we resolved to have pets, not kids.

I grew up with a variety of canine companions and can barely remember my life without a dog in it. My family adopted Samantha, a small, sleek shepherd mix, on my fifth birthday. Although Sam seemed to take pleasure in being around "her people," her demeanor was decidedly cool and patrician. Sam wasn't the kind of pup who'd try to sneak up on the couch next to me. She eschewed the notion of sleeping curled up on the end of my or my brother's bed, instead opting to sleep downstairs on the braided rug by the back door.

Sam was never a jumper, but not because she wasn't capable. In fact, she mastered the ability to fly over our six-foot fence at will, even at fourteen years of age. Rather, I suspect she never pounced all over visitors because it simply wasn't dignified. Ditto on begging for table scraps. If she'd been human, she'd have the Waspy, detached elegance of Grace Kelly or Lauren Bacall. Her dinner would consist of gin, tonic, and cigarettes, and she'd quietly bemoan how Bar Harbor was starting to attract "not our kind, dear."

In terms of play, Sam preferred to entertain herself, thank you very much. At the beginning of every summer, we'd dig out her tennis balls and Frisbees. The second we opened our in-ground pool, Sam would spend hours dropping her toy du jour into the serene blue oasis, then pawing at the water to change the current so that her Frisbee or ball would float back to her in the most expedient manner. We'd try to engage her in games of fetch, but as soon as she caught whatever we'd fling, she'd spirit that item back to the water, thus playing her own version of keep-away.

In my teens, my parents adopted an adorable fluff-ball named Juneau. She was a keeshond mix and embodied everything Sam didn't. Juneau was snuggly, sweet, solicitous, and more than a little stupid. All she wanted to do was be near us and, if it wasn't too much trouble, please have a bite or ten of whatever we were eating.

Juneau loved Sam exactly as much as Sam loathed Juneau.

Sam went so far as to figure out how to open the doggie gate between the family room and breakfast nook, using her pointed nose to close it behind her in an effort to escape Juneau's unbound enthusiasm. Sam lived longer than any dog we've had since, primarily, we believe, out of spite.

After we lost Sam, my parents wanted a purebred. My father's secretary researched farms in the tristate area and my parents opted to do business with the cheapest possible provider.* They brought home George, who grew to be a handsome hundred-and-thirty-pound Great Pyrenees . . . with a taste for my mother's blood. Although I secretly commended him for not tolerating my mother's passive aggression, in all fairness they really couldn't have a dog who actively tried to assassinate her. After extensive work with the vet, a trainer, prescription medication, a shock collar, and a self-titled "doggie psychologist," poor Georgie went the way of the dodo. And Juneau finally grew back all the fur she'd lost on her tail due to stress.

King George's reign of terror was followed by Ted. Ted was a massive purebred Newfoundland who did not want to kill any of my family. In fact, he was so concerned about our safety and well-being that he'd burst through plate glass windows in order to rescue us from the pool. We couldn't curb this behavior, despite our best efforts, and we were terrified he'd hurt himself. Spooked by her experience with George, my mother insisted we return Ted to the breeder. The breeder, in turn, promised Teddy would be sent to a Newfoundland rescue group. But apparently that was too much effort, so the breeder simply put him down for no reason other than the poor dog acting on his instincts.

*The Amish—great cabinetmakers, bad breeders.

I've yet to forgive anyone in this scenario.

Because of my limited, terrible experience with breeders who more than likely were actually puppy mills, I pledged to myself that I would only ever adopt dogs. My parents were equally rattled, deciding that the line of Lancaster dogs would end with Juneau.

After I'd been in college awhile, I adopted an enormous malamute-Akita mix. Nixon was both a gentleman and a scholar, friendly to all walks of life. We'd stroll across campus and students would stop in their tracks to bask in his magnificence. Social and particularly affable, Nick enjoyed going to parties with me almost as much as he liked sharing my bed. This was a mixed blessing. On the one hand, I'd finally gotten my dream of having a dog that'd sleep beside me. On the other, he was a hundred and twenty pounds and I had a twin mattress.

Nixon knew that as soon as I got up to turn out the overhead light, he could jump onto my bed and claim prize sleeping position, so I tried to outsmart him one night. I flipped the switch, and instead of leisurely picking my way through the dark, I dove straight at my bed. But Nick was one step ahead of me and was already in the air when I leapt. This resulted in a minor concussion on my part. After that, I resigned myself to curling up on a quarter of the mattress.

When I brought Nixon to my parents' house for the first time, Juneau was beside herself. She never realized she could meet another dog who *actually liked her.*

She was smitten.

And yet no one was more smitten than my father. The feeling was mutual. When my dad and Nixon were in a room together, it was like no one else even existed. Whereas I'd adopted Nick as my companion, my father found in him a soul mate.* The more time we all spent together, the more I saw that Nixon was better suited to life at my parents' house than at my small campus apartment (and bed).

Nick spent a halcyon week with my folks while I was on spring break, after which my dad told me in no uncertain terms, "Nixon lives here now." I certainly could have argued, but everyone was so happy that it just didn't make sense not to honor the arrangement. Nick lived almost a decade longer than his breed's expected lifespan specifically because he had such a great life full of long walks and daily jaunts into town for sausage biscuits.

My husband's experience with dogs was far more limited. As a child he had a particularly bite-y, highly strung poodle. All he ever wanted was a "proper" dog, like a Doberman or a Rottweiler.† He loved seeing Nixon and Juneau, and each visit to my parents' house strengthened our resolve to get our own.

However, the timing for adoption was all wrong. We were both putting in crazy hours at our technology jobs, and getting a dog made as much sense as getting a neck tattoo. We'd never be home, and we thought our schedules would be so unfair to the dog. Plus, we lived in a fourth-floor walk-up. To perform the simple act of potty, we'd have to go up and down a hundred steps and then walk a block before we got to any grass. Multiply this by four times a day for an adult dog and that was four hundred stairs. I couldn't even imagine how many steps it would take to housebreak a puppy; I'd have to send off to NASA for that kind of math.

---

*Sorry, Mom.
†And if the dog didn't try to hump him while he was on his tricycle, all the better.

Our dream of dog ownership would have to wait until we moved into a bigger place with fewer stairs.

The universe, of course, had other plans.

I lost my high-powered executive position during the dot-com crash of late 2001 and suddenly found myself with an extra sixty hours a week. Try as I might, my job search proved fruitless.* As I had nothing better to do with my time, I started volunteering at a no-kill dog shelter.

At no point did anyone mention this shelter specialized in pit bull rescue, so that was an unexpected, unwanted surprise on my first day. I'll admit I bought into the media's characterization of the breed . . . that is, until I actually worked with them. I couldn't believe how dogs coming from the most abusive situations could still have enough faith in humanity to let us volunteers touch their sweet, scarred muzzles and pet their emaciated bodies.

I met dogs who'd lived through the worst of everything. They'd been beaten and fought and overbred. They'd been fed gunpowder and had bottle caps sewn under their skin so they'd be more aggressive. Some of them had no ears after having been docked not by a skilled veterinarian, but sliced off by their gang-banger owners. Some had huge pink scabs from where they were burned with acid as a punishment for refusing to fight. Yet the minute I'd approach their cages, they'd wag their entire bodies. These poor creatures weren't angry about the past; rather, they were simply grateful for the present. Within a single volunteering shift, pit bulls won me over with their affable personalities, enormous doggie smiles, and innate desire to make humans happy.

I was smitten.

*Feel free to read all about it in my memoir *Bitter Is the New Black*.

So when asked to foster a couple of puppies due to shelter overcrowding, I agreed, but only on a very short-term basis. I mean, although the puppies in question were cute, it wasn't like I could keep them or anything. Seriously, do you know how many stairs that'd mean?

I mean, yes, I'd care for them temporarily, but I wasn't quite ready to change my whole life for them. I was still too selfish. I wouldn't stand for the kind of living beings that could destroy a prize pair of Chanel slingbacks in the ten seconds it took to answer a ringing phone. I wasn't someone who'd make the late-night vet run, shelling out three hundred bucks after the dog had an allergic reaction to the Crème de la Mer she consumed. And I certainly wasn't the kind of person who'd get up at the asscrack of dawn, roll out of bed, and throw on a pair of her husband's sweatpants to take dogs on their first of four hundred daily jaunts outside.

Except apparently I was.

What I forgot that fateful day I agreed to foster the puppies is that no needy creature who enters my house ever leaves. Case in point? The six cranky, elderly cats I'd taken in during college.*

So, much like those couples who find themselves pregnant years before they planned, Fletch and I became dog owners.

All his life, Fletch yearned for a dog that was powerful and smart and obedient. He wanted a noble beast with confidence and quiet dignity and strong lines. When pressed for what kind he wanted, he'd simply reply, "I want an ABP."

"What's that?" I asked.

"Anything But Poodle."

---

*We've since lost four of them to age-related illnesses, but not to worry! I rescued three feral kittens to replace them. But that's a story for a different anthology.

Our puppy Loki fit the bill nicely in looks and personality. He quickly learned to respond to voice and hand commands and seemed to possess an innate intelligence. He had many classic shepherd features, but due to his black fur (save for white patches on his chest and backside) he was more exotic than the garden-variety shepherd. His legs were longer than the breed standard and his chest slightly more narrow. Fletch explained that Loki's leg and chest shape indicate the kind of dog built to plow through snow, so we speculated he was part husky, too. After watching a program on wolves, we determined that Loki was only a few genes away from his lupine predecessors. Because we enjoyed the contrarian notion of having a dog directly descended from a wild animal, we'd tell people he was part wolf.*

Maisy, on the other hand, was the polar opposite of Loki. We knew she was some kind of pit bull terrier, but assumed she, too, had a mixed parentage. Where Loki was long and lean and snout-y, Maisy was short and stocky with a small underbite. We thought maybe there was a little English bulldog in her recent history.† Maisy was tan and white and rounded in all the areas where Loki was dark and angular. She was desperate to connect with people, whereas Loki was mostly interested in other dogs. Loki was obedient, yet with Maisy we quickly learned there's nothing more tenacious than a terrier.

The one thing these dogs had in common was they were absolutely going to be best friends for life.

---

*Years later we'd have a DNA test that showed that Loki is 25 percent Lab and 25 percent poodle. Fletch has protested this finding as firmly as the paternity-tested deadbeat dads on the Maury Povich show.

†Actually, according to her DNA, she's 100 percent American bulldog, a type of pit bull descended from the English bully.

Between all the stairs and the dogs' appetite for designer footwear* and table legs, the first few months of puppyhood were difficult. We worked hard to instill discipline in the dogs, following all the commands dictated in our training books. We did our best to keep the dogs from jumping on people, to teach them to stay off the furniture, and to discourage any kind of begging at the table. And at night, the dogs slept not with us, but with their backs pressed against each other in their side-by-side crates.

After we'd had the dogs for a while, my husband lost his job, too, as part of the whole dot-com fallout. To save money, we moved to a different apartment. Although we weren't thrilled about the downgrade in lifestyle, we were thankful to live in a building with significantly fewer stairs.

The day we moved was long and stressful and disorganized. Fletch and I were ready to drop when bedtime rolled around and neither of us had the energy to assemble the dogs' crates. "I think they'll be fine for one night," Fletch assured me. We set up a pile of blankets and pillows in the corner of the room and then fell into our own bed, exhausted.

When I woke up in the morning, I found myself being spooned . . . only not by my husband. At some point in the night, Maisy had not only climbed onto the bed, but worked her way down under the covers, shoving her broad chest up against my back and resting her sweet face on my pillow.

Here's the thing about pit bulls—their will is stronger than yours, period, hard stop. Once they find something they like, they'll spend the rest of their lives attempting to replicate that action. And now that Maisy had a taste of sleeping in the bed, she

---

*The Chanel slingbacks were a particular favorite.

was not about to ever climb back into that damn crate like a sucker.

And if *Maisy* wasn't sleeping in a crate then *Loki* wasn't, either.

Now this? Right here? Is the exact day the balance of power began to shift in our household.

Sensing our weakness, slowly but surely the dogs began to assert their will. Over time we found that we didn't sit on the couch alone anymore. Sleeping in the bed became a group effort, and eventually we had to upgrade to a king mattress to accommodate everyone. Dinner à deux became a family affair, with dogs casting long and meaningful glances from our plates to forks to mouths, as if to say, "Do you *really* need that last bite of sausage, fatty?" And Maisy, tired of crossing her legs all night to compensate for her unusually small bladder, would occasionally let go on the small braided rug by our back door.*

Oh, we tried to stem the tide of naughtiness, but it turns out I'm not the disciplinarian I thought I was. When I'd point accusatorily to the wet spot on the rug, all it took was a baleful look from Maisy's liquid chocolate brown eyes and suddenly I found myself apologizing to her for making her feel bad. When I'd correct Loki for getting pushy over a bite of my cheeseburger, all he'd have to do was lower his ears and crouch his shoulders. I'd turn into putty in his paws and he'd become the burger king. And Fletch? Although he flatly denied it, Fletch was equally permissive. Perfect example? Cooking them hot breakfasts "because they prefer it."

Years passed and our financial situation improved.

---

*And somewhere in the ether, Sam is shaking her head with a mix of pity and disgust.

The dogs' attitudes, however, did not.

One night six years into our collective lives together, we were watching an episode of *Last Comic Standing*. Fletch and I were shoved into our respective corners of the big couch, while Maisy spread out in the middle and Loki took up the entire love seat. Midway through the show, a comic did a bit about having previously been a teacher's aide. He talked about the effort it took to find something positive to say about children who were *positively* horrible—for example, telling parents their kids had "a lot of energy," which really meant, "Put Junior on Ritalin, stat!"

The bit was funny and we laughed in all the right places, particularly since we continued to find other people's poor parenting a great source of amusement.

We quietly high-fived ourselves on not being responsible for having brought any demon spawn into this world. I sat there ensconced in my smug sense of superiority until I remembered something. Specifically, I recalled how a look of relief washed over the vet tech's face when we announced we were there to claim Maisy and Loki on Saturday after returning from a night out of town.

Now that I think of it, the tech wasn't *smiling* so much as she was gritting her teeth as she practically water-skied behind the tugging, leashed dogs.

When I asked the tech how Maisy and Loki had behaved, she hesitated before she said, "They . . . they felt right at home."

So . . . if the dogs felt right at home, that meant they ignored any attempts at discipline, they jumped on guests, they slept on all the beds and couches, they stole the cats' food, and they peed on the rug in the front hallway.

Oh.

Oh, no!*

I then rooted around in my purse to find the paperwork the tech handed me as we were leaving. They'd prepared a report card of our pets' behavior. At the time, I was proud of the dogs for sailing through their stay, receiving high praise. But upon rereading, I saw that the kennel employed the same practices as the hopeful comedian's old school district.

"Maisy and Loki love to play. They are very excitable and very active."

What I think this actually meant is: *You need doggie Ritalin. Or an exorcism. Possibly both.*

"Both dogs are always on the move. Maisy loves the ball and Loki loves chasing Maisy around."

Seriously, they wore our asses out. WTF is wrong with them? Do you feed them coffee or something?

"They did not engage in group playtime with any other dogs."

Your dogs share exactly the same kind of sociopathic behavior you and your husband exhibit, and we kept them far the fuck away from normal people's pets.

"They both ate well while they were here."

Your dogs are little piggies. Seriously. For reals. Call Jenny Craig, like, now.

"There were no problems with elimination."

Maisy peed on our rug. And in our lobby. And on our porch. But not outside.

That's when it hit us—we'd turned our dogs into the kind of spoiled, entitled, ad hoc children we'd spent so many years rally-

---

*Or, if you're versed in LOLCAT, "Oh noes!"

ing against. And our tidy, orderly home was not only always cha-otic, but often coated in a thin film of fur and slobber. Plus, we never got to sleep in and had to make all our plans around the dogs' needs. Maisy had me so well trained that I knew exactly which yip meant she wanted more water and which meant she was ready for her snack. Strangers and friends alike would raise disapproving eyebrows at our dearth of discipline and co-sleeping habits.

Essentially we'd morphed into the very kind of parents we were always so quick to judge.

We'd become exactly what we promised we'd never be.

And as it turns out, *we didn't care.*

This made us wonder, if we were able to become so cavalier and adaptable about the way in which we raised our dogs, what else were we capable of doing?

And maybe, just maybe, was it possible that our combined DNA *wouldn't* spawn a supervillain?

Of course, we still didn't get neck tattoos.

Because those just look stupid.

Oedipus Rex

Stephanie Klein

I wanted to have a baby, which made my husband shit kittens.

"I want one, too," he said, chasing it quickly with a, "But, first, how 'bout a dog?"

And with this I became convinced that the term "housebreaking" referred not to the act of training a pet to urinate outside, but to the broken home that ensues when a husband defecates on your dream.

For the better part of that week, he continued his "Baby Steps Toward Baby" campaign, reasoning that raising a pup would be an opportunity to break in our parenting skills and establish a division of labor. We'd navigate teething, separation anxiety, and loose stool, all without stretch marks or any need for sex. He assured me the experience would make us strong, united, one—ready to procreate the hell out of each other. And he was right. I hate to admit it, but once we welcomed home Linus, a Toy Fox Terrier pup, everything he'd promised worked out just as planned. You know, aside from our savagely heinous divorce.

Once the husband became my wasband, I moved across town

with our surrogate love child, Linus, explaining that my broken home would always be his broken home.

Then I pointed to the hallway that was my New York City kitchen and told him to poop where he liked. "We're in this shit together now, kid." And that's exactly what the Lineman became, my furkid.

I fell in love with him the way you do at the beginning of things—in the details. I'd mute the TV just to listen to him crunch his kibble in the other room. I loved the smell of his corn chip paws, his proclivity for Dutch ovens, how when his nails got too long his little cleats marched across the wooden floors of our home. I practically shat rainbows over a dog I hadn't even wanted. Funny how it took the dissolution of my marriage for me to find true love, puppy or otherwise.

The Lineman and I became inseparable, hopscotching our way to the West Village in search of choke collars, harnesses, and coordinating leads. Then, we shopped for Linus.

After stocking up on his cable-knit sweaters, we threaded our way to Pastis, grabbing sustenance beneath a red awning on a cobblestone street. It was there, as I cut my steak frites into tiny chewable pieces *for a dog*, that I recognized that the wasband was right. Puppies are exactly like babies. Only cuter.

Aside from the feedings, squeaky toys, vaccinations, and bills, with both dogs and kids, you've gotta air 'em out and run 'em ragged, just so they'll piss off long enough for you to take one. Enter: Puppy Kindergarten.

I laid out Linus's clothes a week before school began. Didn't want the poor thing having nightmares of showing up to school naked. But when his first day arrived, and the forecast threatened rain, I insisted we swap out his fringed suede moccasins for the reflector booties. The Burberry trench was a bit excessive, but Linus begged.

Puddle-jumping across Columbus Avenue, we arrived for his first day at Biscuits & Bath—a multi-floor Shangri-la for the pampered pooch. I removed Linus's booties, handed off the lunch I'd packed, and asked the staffer if she wouldn't mind taking just one last photo.

"Linus, Mama wants a good report," I threatened behind a sad smile. Then the staffer dragged him away, his cleats digging into the turf, the both of us in tears. I watched from a window as he grew smaller in the distance, the whole time his wet face turning back to look for me. In concert with his tears, his knit brow said it all: *Woman, how could you?* The rest of the day, I sat on the toilet.

In time it got easier for him, not me. After puppy kindergarten, he matriculated from obedience and etiquette class and was ultimately granted a bench position in a top socialization meetup group. Though in his yapping, he was adamant that I stop referring to it as a "playdate." Apparently playdates were for puppies and overscheduled children. I had to face facts; he was growing up. Now it was my turn.

In lieu of nights spent retouching our mani pedis, I put myself out there and began to date. Which drove me directly to therapy. Which led to the fetal position. Which, when you think about it, led to some deviant sex. It was like the part of *The Wizard of Oz* where everything turns to color, only with fewer midgets.

Things were good. Perfect, even. Only, I should probably disclose that, during this heyday, Linus mauled one of my bedmates, leaving his face bloody, in need of three stitches. A hiccup, really. At least the guy had the decency to be a doctor and stitch up his own mess.

Okay, fine. Even *I* was beginning to question my parenting skills. Was all this pampering detrimental? After consulting my Magic 8 Ball, I realized it was "Decidedly so." All my mollycoddling was giving sweet Linus a complex—an Oedipus complex.

People say that jealousy isn't a measure of love but a symptom of insecurity. It was obviously why Linus wanted to eat my dates; he was just an insecure, misunderstood poochie-poo. My mission became clear: operation self-esteem, in full effect.

Each morning began with self-affirming mirror mantras, followed by a healthy dose of ABBA. On afternoon walks I made it my business to point out all the uglier dogs. "Look, honey lamb, that one belongs on *Extreme Makeover for Dogs*." We'd fall asleep to audiobooks by Tony Robbins.

Only much to my dismay, things just got worse. My Toy Fox Terrier showed signs of having developed a Napoleon complex. I needed help.

Specialists were roped in, professionals consulted, then I really showed Linus who's boss when we marathon'd our way through Cesar Millan's whispering. So, it *was* my behavior that caused this. Well, then it was going to be my behavior that fixed it.

I went alpha on his ass. It wasn't pretty, but I got him to sleep in his crate. Once a week. Exercise was crucial, but Linus never really took to my elliptical machine. I'd figure out something.

"Something" was yoga. I think it really put things into perspective for Linus. Though, eventually, he did pee his line in the sand. But who could blame him? He obviously found downward-facing dog offensive.

It wasn't until my sister Lea came to visit from Florida that something finally took. Lea and Linus developed what can only be described as an incestuous relationship. Right in front of me, they eye-flirted their way through dinner, eating opposite ends of a single strand of spaghetti, then yawned in sync and retired to my bedroom, where they passed in and out of sleep, staring at each other through the night.

It felt as if I were being displaced by the nanny. I tried to remind myself that Lea was simply a shiny new toy. "Le-anus," as I took to calling them, would be over in a week. If not, I'd threaten to kick Lea in the head and tell God she died.

Of course he adored her. She's a licensed massage therapist, for chrissake. Even bacon can't compete with that. Still, I couldn't begrudge the Lineman her help. She did, through the wonder of puppy massage, seem to cure his hostility and aggression toward my suitors. I don't know what she did to his pressure points, but her magic touch accomplished the job. She taught my old dog not to be jealous when I turned tricks.

Her timing was impeccable, because it was then, a month after she returned to Florida, that my favorite suitor, Philip, fell to bended knee and asked for my hand in marriage.

"Maybe" might not have been the best word choice.

"It's just . . . I have to check with Linus first."

"Stephanie, please don't worry. If he even tries to bite me, I'll bite him back."

My fears were finally allayed when I saw that it was true love betwixt my menfolk. As the only woman in both their lives, I didn't experience the pangs of jealousy I had with Lea. Instead, I thrilled when the dude duo frolicked in the park, drank piña coladas, and liked getting caught in the rain. Only, when it came to Phil and me making love at midnight, Linus began to plan his great escape.

One morning, as the sun filtered through my blinds, thin stripes of it marked across our bodies, Linus let out a Woodstock of a yawn, and we realized he was no longer in his crate. As planned, he'd escaped, sneaky sneaky style, and like a needy child who never wants to be boxed out of the action, he was sandwiched between us—a family of three. It was then that Phil leaned in to kiss me, and Linus leaned in to eat Phil's face for breakfast.

"Holy shit, are you okay?" It was one of my smarter questions.

Thankfully, Phil *was* okay. As okay as you can be when a dog nips at your face. It's why I came to Linus's defense when Phil tried to bite him back.

"Phil, he did it 'cause you got up in his face!"

"No, Stephanie, he did it 'cause he wants to have sex with you!"

He had a point. But at least the damage was minimal. Linus had simply given Philip a Joaquin Phoenix lip.

"I dunno," I said as we assessed the mutilation, "it looks kinda hot. You need to think of this as a slight improvement."

The truth is, I really didn't know what to do. I felt heartsick and anxious and wanted to comfort myself with cheeseburgers. We sat in silence for a while, until Phil finally spoke up.

"That dog is going to chill the hell out once we move to Texas."

Move to Texas—you could almost see the words still hanging in the air when Linus began to weep.

"That's right, who's your daddy now, bitch?" Only Phil didn't actually say this. Had he, it would've been a horribly inaccurate rhetorical question. Not only was it physically impossible for Linus to be a bitch, but Phil also was no daddy.

Not yet.

We moved to Austin, Texas, for the same reasons a dog licks

his balls. Because we liked wet heat. That, and we truly could move anywhere. With my writing scripts and memoir, and Phil in finance, neither of us was tied to a specific location. Austin being the blue part of a red state, Live Music Capital of the World, and a young college town where we'd be welcomed anywhere in flip-flops, we said, "Hell, yes." Only once we actually moved to the Bible Belt, we modified that to, "H-E-double-hockey-sticks, yes." Seeing that "hell" is such a goddamn offensive word and all. We fit right in.

The transition was noticeably harder for Linus, who seemed to be working through the five stages of grief. The denial was obvious from the onset. He refused to be caught dead in a Longhorns sweater and made a point of shrouding himself in head-to-tail black. The anger was harder to detect, but that might've been due to his new muzzle. He apparently skipped the bargaining and headed straight for the depression. R.E.M.'s "Everybody Hurts" played on repeat.

I thought a trip to the local dog park might raise his spirits. Somehow it only served to underscore the disparities between a city dog and a pack of "mongrel hicks"—his words, not mine. I threw a ball, tried to encourage him to play nice, but he wasn't having any of it. When other dogs approached, Linus remained aloof, barking a few times, as if to say, "If I throw a stick, will you just leave?"

"Oh, go on, Linus. They won't bite."

" . . . "

"Fine, I'll go first."

I approached a man whose first name was Bland. He struck me as the type who'd brag that his truck didn't come with seat belts. I'm embarrassed to say that I was wholly off the mark.

He bragged about his trailer. Specifically, the trailer he'd attached to the back of his pickup. Inside were his "bird dogs." Bland was waiting for the last of them—a tricolor beagle—to finish up. Aside from the dogs I'd seen in oil paintings, I never truly associated dogs with anything other than companionship. But after seeing how animated Bland became speaking of his German pointer and retrievers, I realized that to be happy, dogs didn't need bottled water, doggy ice cream, or fleshy raw meats from Lobel's on Madison. Dogs could actually be treated like dogs and still thrive. It was enlightening. So much so that it inspired me to remove Linus's sun visor.

I took a seat on the bench beside my little antisocialist, ready to explain that from now on he was going to be a dog. And dogs are pack animals, which would mean he'd need to get off his rump and hobnob. I knew he wasn't going to like it, so I wanted to be sure my approach was particularly sensitive.

"Dude, stop being such a puss."

And just like that, Linus leapt from the bench and ever so skittishly approached a bulldog in a bandana from behind. With a deep inhale, ready to acquaint himself, Linus suddenly came careening back, skyrocketing through the air into my lap.

"What's wrong with you? You're acting like a freak show!"

"Me?! That redneck's beagle didn't even look for a Wee-Wee Pad; he just did his business on the grass all willy-nilly. I'm sorry, but these dogs are fucking animals!" Or at least that's what I think he said. I didn't write it down.

I told Phil that I was really beginning to worry. I joked a lot, but I genuinely liked the people I'd met in Texas. Sure, I'd prejudge them and think because I was a savvy New Yorker that I was somehow worldlier than, say, a man named after an adjective. But

I was mostly dead wrong. Bland wasn't a redneck. He's a retired oil tycoon . . . who unfortunately lives up to his name. Perhaps he's not my best example of the friends I've made. Point is, I was making them, but Linus just wasn't coming around.

Mid-mopefest he'd sometimes break into a begging howl, as if to say, "I'll do anything; just send me back to a place where the mailman doesn't drive an unmarked Tundra." But Phil pointed out that this was only the grief talking, because dogs don't actually speak. Ah, *this* was the bargaining stage; it just came out of order.

I don't know if acceptance ever truly cropped up for Linus. Though I'll allow that a brief respite from the suffering came in the form of just three consonants: BBQ. I can't say that he preferred smoked beef ribs to New York strip, or sauce from the Salt Lick to Peter Luger, but he at least seemed sated, if not happy.

In the weeks that followed, I held my ground. The designer dog carrier was stowed away, leaving Linus to fend for himself as he walked from the car to his acupuncturist. "Sorry, kid. You're not a baby; you need to learn to do things for yourself." So, like it or not, from then on, Linus had to sniff his own balls.

Just as we were all acclimating to the new state of our union, a fortuitous thing happened. Phil went and knocked me up but good.

With twins.

We rejoiced with family and friends. I shopped for hideous clothes. Phil began to count our savings. We couldn't stop smiling, apart from when I barfed in parking lots, begging Phil to tell passersby that I was pregnant, not drunk. Then we sat down to share our news with Linus.

And he fainted.

This wasn't a beta test, a trial run before the real deal, as it had been with the wasband. This was my life, the one I'd always wanted. And while I was exquisitely thrilled, there was also a sadness that hung on my insides. Linus had nursed me through a divorce, a few hangovers, even more broken hearts. He grew up beneath my covers, sleeping in any body nook he could find. Linus was family, my sweet jumping bean, but he was also a biter. Despite the muzzle and professional help we sought, it would only take one bad moment for everything to change. And it scared the shit out of me. So I went to McDangerous and ate my feelings.

Mine wasn't the only pity party in our cheery family.

"Oh, please. I wish I had your problems," Lea said over the phone. "Try having my life. No boyfriend, crap friends, I'm piss poor—we won't even discuss the fact that I'm a disgusting fat moo who sweats when she breathes." Then, out of nowhere she began to cry.

"You don't have crap friends."

A week later, when Linus saw Lea standing at our front stoop, he nearly shit himself. Instead, he shit the floor and missed the paper. Her bags weren't even out of the car when she let Linus pin her to the ground and have his way with her. He licked up her nose until her brain hurt. Then he raced to our closet, hauled out his designer dog carrier, and promised to write.

He was right. There was one move that would bring everyone happiness.

Now in Florida, a suburb of NYC, Linus is happier than a dog with two peters. He's back to a life of gourmet dog treats, milk and honey baths, and taking up most of the bed. Lea, no longer without a boyfriend, is trying to legalize marriage between humans and animals.

As for me, I really miss him. And a part of me still aches. But it stopped being about me as soon as I had these babies. Thanks to the Lineman, I'm now savoring these moments before my wee ones are led down their own school corridor, turning back to look for me.

Still a family, we Skype regularly, and send a few pounds of Texas beef ribs his way. You could even say that his winding up with an in-house masseuse is his "happy ending," but then you'd just be a perv.

Ménage à Dog

Alice Bradley

My husband, Scott, and I sleep with someone else.

His name is Charlie.

We found Charlie when we were newlyweds and our love was too big to keep between the two of us. One day, while holding hands and surfing the Internet, we spotted an adoption ad for an underweight, abused black-and-white mutt. He might have been part terrier or whippet, but in the picture, his knobby knees and long legs made him look more than anything else like a fawn or baby goat. Like he had just learned to stand. He was chained to a pipe, looking up at the camera with big wet eyes. Below the picture was the following line: "He's just a sweet dog with soft ears who needs a chance." I called. The dog was housebroken, affectionate, and still available. Did we want him? Of course we did.

We picked him up only a few days later, and we were immediately in love. On the walk home, Charlie was thrilled as only a dog can be, his sad past scrubbed clean from his tiny brain. *Walking! Hey! Smells! Wow!* He skittered and barked at parked cars and peed on every available leaf and sidewalk crack that required marking.

Eventually we got home—where he leapt from one piece of furniture to the next and horrified the cats—and then it was time for bed.

This is when we introduced him to his crate.

I hadn't really read up on the latest dog thinking—this was an impulse adoption, after all—but I had grown up with a standard poodle named Molly who, in her earlier years, had been crated, so I figured that that's what you do. He was suspicious of the crate, but we managed to lure him in with treats. He circled the perimeter, whining, sniffing around for an escape route.

"He'll get used to it," I said. "Right?" He was still in our bedroom, after all. And there were blankets in there, from our bed. And squeaky toys! Which, it turned out, terrify him! Whoops!

But as soon as the lights were off, he began to yowl.

Excuse me? Mom? Dad? Did I mention that I call you "Mom and Dad," already? So! Hey! What's up with this prison?

We lay there, listening to him pawing at the metal and whining, and that line from the ad kept coming back to me: *He's a sweet dog with soft ears who needs a chance.*

"Maybe we should let him out," Scott suggested.

Sweet dog. Soft ears. Chance. Needs it.

"Won't that, I don't know, send the wrong message?" I asked.

"Chance" does not mean "locking him in jail." You monster.

"What message?" Scott said.

Charlie cried louder. *Hey, hello? Can someone, you know, save me? Again?*

"I can't remember," I said. "Wasn't there a message we didn't want to send?"

Scott got up and opened the crate, and Charlie leapt onto the bed, scouring our faces with his tongue. "I suppose he can sleep by our feet," I said. "Just for tonight."

On cue, Charlie turned to paw at the sheets. When Scott lifted them, he slid right in and settled down. Charlie had found his place, and it was between us.

We thought this was delightful, that first night. We sandwiched him, stroked his ears, and gazed into each other's eyes. Charlie's trembling quieted. We were his saviors. We were the best people who had ever lived. Our love had rescued this malnourished, frightened dog. Who would eventually feel calm and confident enough to sleep in his crate, or at least in a dog bed, or maybe the couch, or whatever.

But definitely not in the bed with us. Because that would be weird.

It's been eleven years since that first night. Eleven years later, I can count on one hand the number of times we've been home and Charlie has spent a night *not* lying between us, under the covers. He is a permanent nighttime fixture in our bed.

Scott loves that Charlie wants to sleep with "his pack," as he puts it, but I have mixed feelings about the setup. I might not mind his presence as much if Charlie didn't so obviously prefer Scott to me—at bedtime, at least. During the day Charlie gives his love freely to us both, but come night, he is a one-man dog. There is an awkward third wheel in this ménage, and it's me.

Every night, Charlie waits for Scott to get into bed. Once Scott's under the covers, Charlie climbs on him, rests his paws on either shoulder, and licks Scott's face like it's his job. He really digs in. It's hard to watch, but Scott doesn't seem to mind. After their make-out session, Charlie gets under the covers and presses his body against Scott's. Once he's positioned so that his back is suctioned to Scott's chest and his head is directly under Scott's lips, so that his beloved can tilt his head down at any time and give him a smooch on the noggin, he closes his eyes, lets out a satisfied *whumph*, and then rams his pencil-thin legs directly into my solar plexus. After I remove his paws and begin breathing again, I try to adjust his legs so they don't kill me. Eventually I give up and turn over. Encouraged, Charlie then stretches his legs farther until all four paws form a point, thus pushing me away. Sometimes I'll wake up from an unnerving dream to find his four paws poking right into my butt. Other times a paw will find its way into my hair. Or Charlie's dreaming will lead him to patter and thump his paws against my back, like I'm getting the worst shiatsu ever.

As if that's not annoying enough, Charlie must rotate his sleeping placement throughout the night. He starts out under the sheets with us, but within an hour he leaps out, using our heads for leverage to get free of the sheets, then climbing down our bodies to our legs. After lying across our shins for a while, he re-craves our warmth and heads back up over us, pawing at the covers until he's let back in. Scott sleeps right through these maneuvers, but I, a normal human being, wake up if I'm being trampled. To complicate matters further, if I nudge Charlie or interrupt this process in any way, he leaps off the bed. Which you would think would solve the problem, only once he's on the floor, he stands next to the bed, crying, until Scott gives him explicit permission to return. My reassurance means nothing. So I have to wake Scott so he can tell Charlie to come back up so that Charlie can paw at me and step on my soft body parts. All night.

Despite all of this, I might feel differently if I got the snuggle portion of Charlie instead of the pointy parts, or if Charlie immediately burrowed up next to *me* and put his head on *my* pillow with a satisfied sigh. At least sometimes.

When Scott isn't around, there's nothing I want more than a warm body to curl up next to. And that's when Charlie refuses to sleep with me. He seems to feel he's being disloyal. (I'm guessing, of course, because he refuses to tell me outright.) If he agrees to be on the bed at all, it's at the farthest point from me, facing the door, ready to leap up at the slightest hint of a key jangle or a door click.

"He's the same way when you're not here," Scott insists. "He just wants his family together."

My husband, of course, is a liar. I've come home late at night to find the two of them spooning in bed, no bothersome female getting in the way of their union.

My first attempts to cast Charlie from the bed began weeks after we adopted him. Mommy and Daddy needed some alone time, I reminded Scott. Our sexual escapades were being usurped by these platonic cuddle orgies. Scott thought we should schedule our private moments *around* bedtime, because, after all, we didn't want the dog to feel lonely. But even then, Charlie was never far from his thoughts.

"He seems so sad out there," he'd tell me as we snuck away, leaving Charlie curled up on the couch.

"He's asleep."

"All alone."

"He's unconscious. He's not sad."

"But he might wake up, and he won't know where we are."

It doesn't help that Charlie has the saddest face you've ever seen. If you gathered some orphaned unicorns in a room and had them cry into a vessel, the magical being that would mope forth from their basin of tears would look a little less sad than Charlie. Even when he's consumed with joy, his face looks like he's got Gilbert O'Sullivan's "Alone Again, Naturally" on a constant loop in his head. But really, his head is just shaped like that. His brain is probably only playing a series of beeps. Even so, closing the door on him meant him giving us that *look* (which was his normal look) while he trembled (which he does whenever we look at him). If he was in the bed already, we'd have to drag him out, after he spent a few minutes trying to convince us that he could just hang out at the foot of the bed, that he didn't care about whatever shenanigans we were up to. Once we got him out of the room and shut the door, we could hear him in the hallway, waiting for us to finish up.

Despite Charlie's best efforts to keep our bed a relations-free zone, I got pregnant. I had to break it to Scott: The dog would have to get out of the bed, for real this time. Our newborn would probably sleep with us, at least some of the time, and there was no way we could have Charlie burrowing down next to our helpless infant, pushing at our baby's tender flesh with his rough paws. We had to break the dog of the bed habit while I was still pregnant, I said, lest he become so inflamed with jealousy upon the child's birth that he pooped on our pillows or tried to set the house on fire. I wasn't so clear on what sign his jealousy would take, but I knew it wouldn't be good.

Besides, as a pregnant woman, I was increasing daily in girth, achiness, and difficulty in getting to sleep. I was growing less and less tolerant of the dog poking and nudging me so he could get fondled by my husband. There wasn't enough room for me, my husband, Charlie, my full-length body pillow, my snacks (sometimes there were snacks), and the fetus.

Scott agreed, reluctantly, but every time we banished him from the bedroom Charlie scratched at the door and wept. We purchased a dog bed and put it by ours. He sometimes used it during the day, but otherwise he regarded it as little better than the crate. Even on the nights I successfully got him off the bed, when I woke up in the morning he'd be there in between us, his head on Scott's pillow, the two of them snoring away. Then he'd stretch out and stick his paw in my eye.

When our son Henry was born, I knew that would be it. Charlie would have to get used to that dog bed, because there was no way he was getting on the bed if the baby was there. Only Henry didn't like to sleep with us. It seemed he and Charlie had reached an understanding when we weren't looking: Henry would sleep in his crib, and Charlie wouldn't eat him.

Whenever Charlie licked Henry's face, Scott would say, "Aw, he loves him!" but I think it was a reminder. *I like the taste of baby, kid. I like it just fine.*

My efforts to free us of Charlie as bed partner redoubled when one night we were awakened by a horrible *glug glug glug* sound and a meaty aroma. We turned back the sheets and found, between us, a hot puddle of dog vomit, and Charlie burrowing ever deeper in the sheets, unapologetic, looking for a clean place to relax. As we changed the sheets, I figured this was my chance to finally get the dog out, once and for all.

"That's it," I said. "He sleeps in the dog bed."

"On the other hand," Scott replied, "he might as well come back in now. It's all out of him."

And then Charlie leapt in between us, in the new clean sheets, while the two commenced making out, Scott murmuring, "You feel all better now, don't you, boy?"

The next night Scott called for Charlie to join us in bed.

"Honey," I said, "do you want to wake up again at three a.m. to change the sheets? Because I really don't."

"That was a fluke," he said. "It's never happened before—what makes you think it will happen again?"

It's happened at least three more times. Countless other times he's started to get sick, but I've become adept at tossing him from the bed at the first sign of any pre-sickness restlessness. This probably means I don't ever fully go to sleep. I'm always on watch, on the alert for potential dog sick. Sleep deprivation takes years off your life. My dog is killing me.

Charlie is thirteen now, at least—his exact age remains a mystery—so lately my efforts to get him out of the bed are met with the argument that he doesn't have much longer and his last few years should be happy ones. This one always gets me. It's true, of course. There's going to come a time, and it may be soon, when I'm going to miss being prodded in the butt by Charlie's paws. Charlie's face has turned from mostly black to gray. Scott has grayed just enough to match his dog.

Sometimes I'll come in and I'll see my two gray-haired men sleeping on their respective pillows, both of them snoring away.

I shove Charlie over, and take my place.

There's No Place Like Home, Judy

Alec Mapa

If you live a good life, you get to come back as a gay couple's dog.

Trust me, Mother Teresa is a Shih Tzu living on the Upper East Side wearing a Dolce & Gabbana trench and having her crap picked up by Uncle Steve and Uncle Dave.

Don't believe me?

My husband and I have two dogs, Ozzy and Sweet Pea, both of whom have a holistic dentist who makes quarterly house calls to clean their teeth.

She's called "The Tooth Fairy."

I shit you not.

I have the canceled checks to prove it.

Ozzy and Sweet Pea fulfill my own mortifying need to be shamelessly affectionate in a way I simply can't be with people.

I have the restraining orders to prove it.

My own husband, after one too many kisses, will repel me with a flexed foot. My dogs are the only living creatures on the planet whose need to love and be loved comes as close to being bottomless as my own. At the end of every day, I am greeted at the front door as if I am a long-lost friend who, mistakenly, was believed to have been dead for years. I sometimes want to tell my dogs that I am undeserving of this avalanche of affection, but I can't bring myself to break the bad news. Besides, I need this illusion of greatness to go on living. Their nightly greeting has made bad auditions, lousy performances, and lonely, loveless days evaporate instantly.

In return, they get *everything*: ergonomically designed chew toys, gourmet treats, and a groomer so skilled she makes Vidal Sassoon look like a butcher.

Ozzy is a cairn terrier. He was an actor who worked on a popular network sitcom. He used to double for his brother. He was identical to him in every way except his metabolism. He got fired for getting fat.

Los Angeles can be a mean, nasty town.

An animal trainer on the lot introduced me to Ozzy and said, "This one's kind of depressed. All his friends at the kennel go to work every day, so he's all alone, and hasn't worked in six months. That's three years to you and me."

I immediately felt his pain.

When Ozzy came to live with us, he was like a Stepford dog.

Ozzy could perform every standard dog trick from "play dead" to "speak" with just a wave of my hand.

It was creepy.

Neither my husband nor I made him do a single thing to amuse us.

Now he sleeps all day and eats his own poo.

I recently did the old "rollover" gesture just to see if he remembered, and he responded by audibly farting then leaving the room.

The most effort that dog will make for the rest of his life will be to move from one comfortable spot to the next.

Of course, I'm jealous.

My husband and I were watching *The Wizard of Oz* one night (because we're gay) when Toto, cinema's most recognizable cairn terrier and Dorothy's iconic dog, made an appearance. We pointed to the screen and said, "Look, Ozzy! It's you!"

In our imaginations, we instantly became convinced that Ozzy truly believed he was Toto, that he actually appeared in *The Wizard of Oz* next to Judy Garland, and, as a result, calls everybody Judy.

We speak his thoughts aloud constantly.

He sounds like an adolescent Mr. Magoo: affable and friendly, yet strangely formal.

We believe his playful woofs and snorts translate into:

"How was your day, Judy?"

"Know what I did, Judy?"

"I just ate some poo, Judy."

"Can you smell it, Judy?"

"You will when I kiss you, *Ju-day!*"

We think this is hilarious.

On a two-week trip to Berlin one summer, we spent the entire vacation speaking to each other in Ozzy's voice.

"Hey, there's the Reichstag, Judy."

"Nice bratwurst, Judy."

"Ich bin ein Berliner, Judy."

We could actually feel the already reserved German population physically pull away from our presence.

Our other dog is a dachshund-Chihuahua mix. A "Dox-iewawa" or a "Chi-weenie," if you will.

We named her Sweet Pea, after the *Project Runway* designer. Because we're gay.

A neighbor had rescued her and thought that we (my husband and I, and Ozzy) would be a good fit.

The first night in our house she cried nonstop.

Sweet Pea was always affectionate and well behaved, but the whining cry was so hideous, it sounded as if she were being tortured.

I don't know if you've ever heard a Chihuahua mutt cry, but it's like squealing tires.

Only not as melodious.

Like someone decided to peel out of a driveway then changed his mind and stopped.

Then decided to peel out again.

Then changed his mind.

You get the picture.

Try listening to that for forty-eight hours.

I got it, okay?

Still, I understood why: She was terrified.

She didn't know whether she was going to be abused or adored. In essence, she was me right before doing stand-up.

I immediately felt her pain.

My husband not so much.

He wanted her out.

Fast.

So, I argued on her behalf.

"She doesn't know where she is! She's scared!"

My husband shot back, "I don't think she's good for Ozzy."

I hated to admit he was right, but Ozzy's always agreeable demeanor had turned into a nonstop vibe of "WTF, Judy?"

After a very heated argument in the car, I had resigned myself to giving her back.

But when my husband and I opened the front door, we saw Sweet Pea in the fetal position, curled up against Ozzy, as if she were seeking sanctuary in his fur.

It was the cutest thing either of us had ever seen.

I firmly believe that while we were out, Sweet Pea sniffed the down doggie bed, the human-grade kibble, the organic herbal treats, and arrived at the conclusion that living with a gay couple was the equivalent to winning the lottery every hour for the rest of her life.

I'm positive the position we found her in was planned.

And it worked.

My husband changed his mind instantly.

To this date, Sweet Pea sleeps every single night directly on top of my husband's neck or in the crook of his balls.

She hasn't whined since.

Everyone wants Sweet Pea.

I've seen the most hardened bitter queens melt in her presence.

A recent dinner guest asked, "What do I have to do to take Sweet Pea home with me?"

I said she'd have to pry her from my cold dead hands.

And I mean it.

Because Sweet Pea has the pleading, doe-eyed look of a pooch in a sixties Keane painting, we've endowed her with the foulest, most inappropriate voice ever. She sounds like Paula Deen with Tourette's syndrome.

"How y'all doin', motherfuckers? Where's my goddamn breakfast, bitch?"

We admonish her profanity.

"Sweet Pea! Is that any way to talk?"

She responds flippantly, an affirmative in two syllables: "Yay-yes."

To the uninitiated, we look insane: two grown men speaking as anthropomorphized dogs.

But lately I've discovered that all dog lovers have a dog voice. I know a woman whose dog voice is actually a wordless, nonsensical theme song that can only be described as a musical mash-up of *Bewitched* and *Gilligan's Island*.

That woman is a district attorney.

Sometimes, Sweet Pea has doggie nightmares.

I watch her squirm and twitch convulsively.

I imagine she's reliving her former life.

Not the one as a rescue, the lifetime before that: the one that earned her all the Isaac Mizrahi sweaters and American Apparel hoodies.

The one where she was a selfless missionary running a leper colony.

Surrounded by oncoming death and disease, she tirelessly cares for the doomed.

"How will I survive this? Will there be an end that justifies this ongoing hell? Holy shit, did I just pull off someone's hand?"

I wake her up.

"It's all right, baby. Daddy's here. Ssshhh."

Momentarily startled, she blinks at me, but then quickly gets her bearings, shakes off the sleep, and takes in her luxurious surroundings. From across the room, Ozzy looks from her to me and says, "Sounds like someone was having a bad dream, Judy."

He heaves a sigh with his entire body, then immediately drifts off to sleep himself, chanting, "It was only a dream, Judy. Only a dream."

The Lone Wolf

Laurie Notaro

I had never seen such a sad look on a dog's face before.

She sat alone in the play yard, not a soul around, hunched under a Fisher-Price play structure. Everyone else, apparently, was inside the doggie day-care center as the lone little dog looked on at the closed door that separated her from her compatriots, forlorn, abandoned, friendless.

It was a pitiful, wrenching sight.

Especially because the dog I was looking at was my very own.

As soon as I hurriedly parked my car, I ran inside the lobby and immediately accosted Sarah, one of the dog wranglers, a cute, perky girl in her early twenties.

"Maeby is out there all by herself!" I boldly proclaimed, pointing in the direction of the play yard, as if there was a nefarious-looking man in a trench coat about to lure my dog away from her position under the plastic log cabin with a laced chicken strip.

The girl smiled. "Oh, Maeby hides," she said comfortingly.

My dog? I thought. She can't be talking about my dog, who howls every time we leave the house to bring her pack back together and who acts like she took a hit off the doggy crack pipe as soon as we pull into the day-care parking lot. I don't know how many Maebys there were at day care, but certainly, she couldn't be talking about *my* dog.

"I mean *my* Maeby," I tried correcting her. "The tan and white Aussie mix, one brown eye, one blue."

She laughed. "Oh, I know Maeby," she said with a wider smile. "There are a lot of times we can't even get her to come inside with the other dogs. She's a little lone wolf."

I almost burst out laughing. She had to be kidding. My Maeby? My little dog, who couldn't wait to burst through the day-care doors in the morning to play with all of her friends? I felt like Sarah had suddenly told me that my dog was a cat or that I had been taking a bonobo on walks all this time. The thought that my dog was a lone wolf was preposterous; we had done everything possible to socialize her before the Experience Window of Doom shut and apparently locked at sixteen weeks. She loved other dogs; in fact, she had been made a doggie day-care "greeter" a year before, in which she was introduced to new dogs to play with them and make them feel at home.

I simply did not believe that my dog was basically skulking around the playground by herself, not associating with anybody and hanging out alone in the log cabin as a matter of choice and preference like Ted Kaczynski.

I knew it was a lie.

Until Sarah opened the door to the play yard and called for Maeby to come in.

She refused to move, looked at us briefly, and then, carelessly, looked away.

Like a lone wolf. Like she didn't even know me.

I gasped.

Sarah glanced at me with an "I told you so" face and headed out to the playground to try and coerce my antisocial dog into coming inside and going home, armed with a cookie that had sprinkles on it.

I told my husband what happened as soon as I got home, and he had as much trouble believing me as I did Sarah.

"She probably didn't feel very well today," he said, trying to explain it away. "That dog is a player. Other dogs line up to play with her. She's been invited to ten dog birthday parties this year alone. Lone wolves lick themselves in public and pee on everything, rub their noses on windows. They don't get invited by every little dog on the block to their birthday parties. She's an A-lister. A must-have."

"That's true, that's true," I said, nodding, mainly because I very much wanted to believe it, but then suddenly had an idea. I ran to my purse and dug out the Doggie Daily, the report card that the day care provided when I picked Mae up.

"Look," I said to my husband after I opened it and read it. "It says here that she was 'a big flirt' today and that she was voted the 'most uplifting.'"

"I saw one from last week around here," my husband said, scouring the coffee table. "Here it is. Oh. Well, look at that. See? Last week she was voted 'most affectionate' and was Dog of the Day. *Dog of the Day.* No one just hands that out. That's equivalent to being the Lord of Dogland. Our dog reigned for an entire day. She could have made policy and waged wars with a kennel or pet resort in a neighboring town. She's like Queen Elizabeth I if the monarch eagerly ate her own eye boogers and became visibly upset when having dirt clods plucked from her belly."

"Uplifting *and* affectionate," I stressed. "I mean, that's pageant-winning qualities, right? *Uplifting?* Have you ever met an *uplifting* dog before?"

"Shall I introduce you to one?" my husband said, motioning to Maeby, who twitched as she lay on the carpet, sleeping.

"Then why is she getting picked last for the kickball team?" I wondered aloud. "I think we have another Doggie Daily on the fridge!"

I ran to the kitchen, plucked it off the front, and was immediately disappointed.

"Voted 'softest hair,'" I reported with a scowl as I walked back into the living room. "*'In the world.'* Big deal. What does that even mean? I can't work with that. That's just filler. Oh—*oh!* But in the 'When I grow up I want to be' section, it says 'write a novel.' Well, how about that? Another writer in the family."

I beamed until I looked up and saw my husband's face.

"Well," he said simply, "there you go. There's your red flag. I don't know how much more you need than that. Clearly, there's something wrong with the dog."

I looked at Maeby, now snoring deeply. How could she have gone from helping transition the new dogs as a "greeter" in day care to the "loner" in what seemed like seconds flat? What could have happened in her little doggie world to spur such a dramatic and sudden change?

I spent the next week wondering if there had been an incident at snack time, or maybe there was a squabble over a chewy or fur was shed regarding a squeaky toy that had Hamlet's territory clearly splattered all over it. Perhaps she peed on a spot that had just been freshly marked by Lola or Baci and it wasn't quite all the way dry yet. Maybe my little mixed dog wasn't welcome on a playground full of purebreds or dogs with papers. The doggie day-care world suddenly seemed like a cruel and dangerous place, full of politics, revenge, and alliances, like a maximum security rec yard or *The Real Housewives of New Jersey*. Things, I realized, could get real crazy real easy. You're Queen Elizabeth one week and then you're on a reunion show in a low-cut dress, and the next, someone has a copy of your felony arrest record and the camera is panning to your mug shot.

My poor dog, I thought as I looked at her sleeping. The heights you have soared; the lows you have seen.

Against my better judgment, my husband took her to day care the next week. I spent the hours worrying that she was hiding out under the slide of the plastic fort, shunned and scorned for the $6.75 I was paying for her to have a fun time. When the clock hit five p.m., I shot out the door to pick her up. When I got there, all of the dog wranglers were in the playroom with their charges, so I pulled Maeby's Doggie Daily from the bulletin board and opened it up. It was there that I found out Maeby, according to the boxes that were checked, spent the day apparently being "howling hot and" "canine cool," and "flirting with her boyfriend, Sammy Schnoodle."

Her *what*?

I still had my mouth open when Sarah walked into the lobby with Maeby on her leash.

"This whole thing," I stuttered, "was over a boy?"

She looked puzzled. I pointed to the Doggy Daily.

"The lone wolf," I explained. "Was playing hard to get? It wasn't because she was exiled from the dog kingdom, which she once ruled like the Shah of Iran?"

"Maeby, an outcast?" Sarah asked, and then burst out laughing. "Oh, hardly. Her milk shake is in the yard. In fact, it spills over quite a bit when she's shaking it."

"I don't understand," I replied, completely confused. "Last week she was all by herself in the yard, and you said she was a lone wolf."

"Oh, last week she was," Sarah agreed, "because she's picky. She just turned three, so she's not a frolicky puppy who will play with just anybody anymore. She's definitely developed some opinions of certain dogs, who she likes, and who bugs her. She only hangs out with who she wants to hang out with. Sometimes that means she doesn't feel like hanging out with anybody."

And just like that, it made sense. I was the one who got picked last for the kickball team, I was the one who oftentimes sat on the playground by myself when I was in school. Who knows where I would have ended up if I had a hardier ability to grow facial hair and got a passing grade in chemistry? Maybe in a log cabin in Montana, maybe inventing Healthy Choice frozen dinners and wearing a chin net.

But the truth of the matter was that Maeby was not me; she was clearly her own little dog, with her own set of likes and dislikes and choices about how she spent the glory of her dog days. Maeby was a milk shake; at her age, I was a lunchroom pint of lukewarm skim milk, opened and hyperactively torn on the wrong side. In the land of doggie day care, I realized, there is no kickball team, there is no dog kingdom, there is no snubbing at snack time. There are just dogs and buttholes, and if someone wants to hang out in a log cabin all by herself, nobody cares, no one notices, and no one talks about it afterward. There will always be a new butt to sniff, and old butts you've already visited.

And in the world of anything, that was certainly most uplifting.

The Evil Stepmother

Jane Green

I liked his smell. I liked the way he walked, and his large patrician nose. I liked the way that whenever I couldn't figure out how to do something—put up the inflatable slide, unblock the sink—he would run over in a flash, and calmly fix whatever needed to be fixed, with his blue eyes twinkling as I made him coffee. I liked that he loved animals and children, and in particular, *my* children: four of them, all under six.

I had been living on an old, old farm in the middle of nowhere in rural Connecticut, when my marriage, already slipping through our fingers like sand, ran out. We had moved to the farm in a rush of romantic fantasies: I would plant orchards, grow our own fruit and vegetables; our children would frolic barefoot and grow up with the many animals we would have: chickens, goats, miniature sheep.

The morning I listened to my then husband's truck pull out of the driveway, the morning after the fight that couldn't be fixed, I knew my life would no longer be that of a farmer's wife. Frankly, I was ever so slightly relieved. All that bread baking and jam making had added a few unwanted pounds, and truth be told, I was terribly lonely out there in the country. It was time to head back to the beach, to be closer to my friends, my support system, as I attempted to adjust to a new life as a single mom.

I rented a tiny cottage by the water in Westport, Connecticut, and promptly fell head over heels in love with living by the beach. Shortly thereafter, I fell head over heels in love with the landlord, he of the twinkly blue eyes, as he fixed the plumbing and took me on long rides on his Vespa.

He and his two children instantly became part of our large family. We had visions of us living happily ever after, almost immediately talking about building a house together, assuming, *knowing*, that we were both in for the long term: the modern-day Brady Bunch.

I thought I'd met every member of the family until the day he drove out from New York in his old truck, parking it in the driveway to come inside for lunch. I went out to get something from the mailbox, and as I walked past the truck, lost in a daydream, a huge noise started up.

I jumped and backed away, terrified, as a snarling mass of fangs and saliva threw its huge bulk at the back window, barking ferociously, revealing huge teeth that looked all the better to eat me with.

I like dogs. Secretly, though, I prefer cats. There was a very good chance that had Landlord not come along when he did, I might have turned into the Crazy Old Cat Lady, somewhat along the lines of Big Edie in *Grey Gardens*. I would happily have lived in a faded old mansion with a hundred cats and the odd tame raccoon (but my bed would have been bigger).

I like the *idea* of dogs very much. I like the idea of a constant companion, an intelligent, playful friend, the unconditional love you get from a dog, and I am not unfamiliar with dogs.

I grew up with Stanley, a standard long-haired dachshund. He was gorgeous to look at, rather grumpy, completely obsessed with my mother, and entirely uninterested in the rest of us. I wasn't hugely interested in him, either, but he proved invaluable as an excuse to go and chat up boys in the local pizza joint. I do remember showing up at said pizza joint one day, and Number One Crush asking what I was doing there.

"Just walking the dog." I feigned nonchalance.

"Where is he?" Number One Crush, not unreasonably, asked, poking his head out the door and looking up and down the street, expecting to see a dog tied to a lamppost.

I had forgotten him. Stanley was at home.

I like dogs like Stanley. Fluffyish is good, scruffy even better. I have a particular penchant for sighthounds; Scottish deerhounds and the rather more elegant Russian wolfhound, the borzoi, are my favorites. I like dogs with hair.

That day, after walking past Landlord's car, then leaping up in terror as the thrashing canine mass tried desperately to break the windows and get out to wrap his huge jaws around my delicate neck, I went running inside, heart pounding as I leaned breathlessly against the door.

"What the *hell* is that?" I heaved.

"That? Oh, that's Baron. He's a mush." Landlord grinned, inviting me out to meet the other great love of his life.

Baron is a Doberman pinscher. He is not just any old Doberman pinscher; he happens to be a genetically modified freak of a Doberman pinscher, who is thirty percent oversized. This means he is actually far more similar to the size of a Great Dane. He is very handsome, with a regal ridge on his head, and, unless you are walking past Landlord's car, which Baron happens to be guarding, he is enormously loving.

A Doberman pinscher, however, was not in my future. *He is not my dog,* I said to Landlord in no uncertain terms, as he navigated the complications of splitting his time between his New York City apartment and our house in Connecticut, making the dreadful commute by car, with Baron tucked up in the back. I liked Baron very much, but I did not want him full-time.

A thirty percent oversized Doberman pinscher, who has spent his entire life ruling the roost, is not an easy dog to inherit. He is so large he can climb up and reach anything. Loaves of bread wedged onto high shelves are nothing for Baron. Fruit pies cooling on wire racks at the very back of the stove disappear in seconds.

Before I came along, Baron spent his nights sleeping alongside Landlord, his huge weight—120 pounds—pressed against his master's side, their breathing in sync as he laid heavy paws on Landlord's sleeping body, emitting evil smells as gas became an increasing problem.

Before I came along, Baron had a dog runner who collected him every day and ran him in Central Park. I will admit, walking him in the city was fun, particularly at night, when our neighborhood on the Upper West Side loses something of its charm and the seamier side of life comes out to play. Crowds of sketchy-looking men in hoodies part like the Red Sea when Baron and I come to pass, and I clutch him tight, as if he would, at any moment, lunge for their hearts.

They do not need to know that if he were to lunge, it would likely be to lean on their legs, pressing his giant head against their stomachs for a long pat.

I did not want Baron full-time. But Landlord became Husband, and slowly, despite my best efforts, I got Baron. First, for a few nights at a time, then it seemed silly for him to go back and forth to his city apartment, particularly when we have a huge yard, and live by the beach, and have children at home, who love nothing more than playing with him.

As in all good stepfamilies, we have a complicated relationship. I am lucky in that he doesn't resent me for taking his father away from him, nor does he scream that he hates me and I have ruined his life. In fact, he adores me for being the one who usually feeds him, the one who opens the door for him, the one who allows herself to be dragged along the beach for his "walks."

They say the key to happiness is not getting what you want, but wanting what you have got. I would never have chosen Baron. He is too large, too unwieldy, too exuberant. And yet, over time we have bonded, and he is now part of this huge, chaotic, exuberant family. I may not want to admit it, but he fits, and I have grown to love him, and to love the joy he brings us.

At the end of every day, when the school bus pulls up at the end of the road, Baron sits up, ears alert, stub of a tail wagging, racing to the edge of the property and panting with excitement as the children climb off the bus. They drop their backpacks and race over to him, slipping small arms around his large girth and hugging him as he leans into them.

They grab balls and fling them across the yard for him. He bounds in circles like a puppy, collapsing at our feet with a smile—and yes, this Dobie actually smiles—laying his head on our shoes.

He is now almost nine, the last of his littermates to survive. He is becoming creaky, slower, less tolerant of men in trucks who do not have a healthy supply of dog biscuits under the dashboard. I, too, am finding myself becoming creaky, slower, and less tolerant of . . . everything.

Baron and I have found something in each other that neither of us expected. He went from living in a small apartment, being on his own for most of the day, to having a huge yard, people at home all day, hordes of children to play with. He knows what it is to chase squirrels, to be thrown dog biscuits by all the UPS and FedEx men, to have neighborhood dogs unexpectedly show up in the yard for impromptu playdates. He has discovered another, happier way of life.

I went from the loneliest of marriages to the unexpected joys of a second chance at love and life: a wonderful husband and partner, a huge blended family, a beach house filled with family, friends, and food. I know what it is to feel loved, and supported, and safe, to live in a community of wonderful people who drop in for cups of tea or glasses of wine. I, too, have discovered another, happier way of life.

And so, those moments when Baron tears through the house barking at the cats, who hide, scowling and hissing, under the sofa, or I walk into the kitchen to find he has managed to knock over the bread bin and has eaten a dozen everything bagels, fresh from the bakery (and really, who can blame him?), my irritation is minor.

We may not have chosen each other, Baron and I, and I may not always have the time I would like to devote to him, but it is enough that we have become part of the fabric of each other's lives, part of the happiness that both of us, later in life, have been lucky enough to find.

Scratching at My Door, Tail Between His Legs

Caprice Crane

"He has my eyes."

"I can't argue this with you," I'd say.

"You can't keep him from me," he'd reply. "He's my son. It's not *fair*."

"I'm sorry you feel sad and alone, but you dug your own grave."

"You're hot when you get angry."

"You still don't get to have him."

"Can I get visitation rights?"

"Maybe," I'd finally give in—a bit. "When it's convenient for me."

"So it's just like my visitation rights with your naked body when we were together."

"Exactly like that, but more enjoyable for me."

He'd add a final dig: "Well, there's another difference . . . Max is actually *fun* to be around."

*   *   *

That's how the conversations would go.

And that's how they'd usually end.

Ugly.

But, truth be told, by the end, our love for Max was the only thing we had in common. And I couldn't blame Colin that much for seeking visitation rights. He'd fallen just as hard as I had. The problem is, during the time we were together, he'd also fallen for many other women. It took me a while to figure out the guy would fall more often than a one-legged man learning to ice skate. At least in Max's case, Colin didn't fall in love behind my back. Or delete his texts to Max so that I wouldn't find them. Or arrange to meet Max when I was out of town, or at work, or filling out my taxes, or painting the apartment, or asleep, or breathing.

Yes, Colin was a bit of a dog himself.

But I knew Colin's love for Max was genuine. How could it not be? Max has that effect on people.

Not that Max is what you would call a "good dog." He's a Shih Tzu, which is Tibetan for *pain in the ass*. For as long as Max has been alive, he's been testing the boundaries of what is edible and what will result in a two-thousand-dollar vet bill coupled with an endless stream of my tears. If you look away for the briefest of moments, he will steal whatever is on your plate. And, sometimes, the plate. Once, I swear, he stole an entire bottle of ketchup from the table. I found it seven months later, empty, in the closed tank of the toilet. I didn't ask.

Max's unparalleled love for and commitment to playing fetch would make you think he was a retriever trapped in the wrong body. (Think Chaz Bono, age sixteen.) And Max's uncanny ability to MacGyver his way into my purse, the trash can, or an unreachable shelf makes me think that somewhere under his soft fur, there's a secret pair of opposable thumbs. Or maybe four pairs. I'm telling you, some of his antics are downright unbelievable.

Then again, those weren't the only unbelievable antics going on in my apartment. (I mean, Facebook was not invented for that purpose. Shame on you, Colin.)

If I added up the years' worth of vet bills and the price of replacement items I've been forced to purchase, Max has probably cost me a lovely vacation home on the Iberian Peninsula. But I can't get angry with Max. Oh, I've tried. But the truth is—unless you catch them right in the act of misbehaving—dogs don't know what you're mad about.

And when Max tilts his head and gives me that familiar "I don't understand you" look, kind of like how Sarah Palin looks when a reporter asks her a question, I just melt. (It's a cute look when it's a dog, and if you're a middle-aged, potbellied Republican from Kansas, you probably think it's a cute look for Sarah Palin, too.)

Anyway, how can I punish him? In his mind, wasn't the box of uncooked oatmeal that he tore open, spread around my entire apartment, and ravenously devoured to the extent possible before I returned simply a delicious (if a bit chalky) feast? It's not like he hasn't seen me tear into a pint of Ben & Jerry's.

Half the time I can't help but laugh when I walk into a room and find Max headfirst, hind legs off the ground, half buried (and now stuck) in a bag, backpack, or briefcase in which he was attempting to find a hidden snack. I can't count the times I've been packing a suitcase for a trip, left the room, and returned to find Max hiding in my luggage, avoiding eye contact and lying perfectly still so I won't notice he's trying to stow away. (Note to Max: The TSA won't allow a four-ounce bottle of moisturizer in my carry-on, so there's no way your Tasmanian devil ass is getting through JFK.)

So when I say he's not a "good" dog, I guess I mean he's one of the best dogs you'll ever have the pleasure to meet. That's even with all of his peculiarities, and probably because of them. Just as people fall for each other not because of the perfections but the imperfections, such is the case with this lovable scamp. Add his charm, his loyalty, his perfect heart, and his magnificent face (including the most stunning underbite you'll see this side of *Sling Blade*) and you have a perfect storm of awesome.

Admittedly, I've always been a dog person. I'm the type who harasses strangers with dogs on the street because I need to say hello to their dog.

Every. Single. Time.

You know, like a child or someone with OCD, who may or may not be able to refrain from warning a stranger that she wants to "eat that dog's face."

(Dog people understand this. At least the ones who don't walk away quickly, mumbling something into their phones about "911" and "devil eyes" and "please hurry.")

That's not to say I dislike animals of other varieties—quite the opposite is true. When I was in high school, I had what could nearly qualify as my own personal zoo. I had two dogs, one snobby cat (she'd always look at me like I was boring her—I probably should have named her Colin), two mice named Sid and Nancy (Sid ultimately killed Nancy—I know, I should have seen that coming), a canary, a chameleon, and a fire-bellied toad named Hank.

While I adored each and every one of those other beings, none of them provided the joy and unconditional love that my dogs did.

And none ever tried to stow away in my luggage or school backpack. (Well, maybe the chameleon did. It was hard to tell.) So as I grew up—look, just play along on the growing-up part—I ultimately gravitated toward dogs for my animal companions of choice.

I rescued Max. Literally rescued him from a shelter in the scary land of hipster Brooklyn and brought him safely to Manhattan, where he would be less compelled to drink Pabst Blue Ribbon beer while donning skinny jeans and shrunken blazers. And for the past ten years, Max has remained my steadfast companion through thick and thin, multiple moves between L.A. and New York, and a handful of ne'er-do-well boyfriends.

Speaking of . . . Colin and I began dating when Max was eight. It was a long-distance relationship that quickly became a short-distance relationship in the form of us moving in together. Colin and Max got along famously, but then again it isn't hard to get along with Max. Max loves everybody and everybody loves Max—that's just a fact, even if you're not a "smaller dog person." Eventually, once exposed to the wonder that is Max, you will fall hard and fast.

This is because he's a giant beast of love trapped in a small dog's body. Don't get me wrong—he's not a purse dog, not that there's anything wrong with that. (A purse tarantula, on the other hand: not cool.) He's not a punting dog, he's not a yelping dog, and he's not one of those super-miniature dogs that looks like a big rat. Max just isn't large. In appearance, at least. His personality is gigantic.

And so began the love affair between Colin and Max. Colin would take him for walks. Colin would take him to have cigars with "his boys." Colin would take photographs of him from every angle at every time of the day and share them with his family as if Max were our child. And, well, he *was* our child.

But only for as long as we were together.

This is the part Colin couldn't wrap his head around. When we broke up, he started to make demands.

"That dog is my son. My only child. I need to see him," he'd argue at every conceivable opportunity. My friends would argue it was just Colin's way back into me—er, I didn't mean that quite the way it sounded. Honestly, I never doubted that Colin genuinely wanted Max time. I just didn't want any more Colin time.

"Yes," I would explain. "He was *our* dog when we were together . . . but he is no longer your dog. Had we gotten Max together, I would see your side, but I had Max for eight years before you came along and I will now (God willing) have him for at least eight more."

"Here's the thing," he'd reply. "You make a point. However, it's not a good one. Max and I are close now. It doesn't matter when you got him. He and I have a bond. We've been through things together. Namely . . . putting up with you. We're like Vietnam vets, or Lady Gaga's parents. We've . . . suffered."

"You mean you shared the *pleasure* of my company." (I was never great at comebacks under pressure.) "Max was the bonus that came along with me. You blew it with me . . . therefore, you do not get to keep the bonus. There is no severance package."

"You can't keep him from me," he'd argue. "He wants to see me, too."

That argument always got to me. Mostly because it was true. Max genuinely loves Colin. But, I reminded myself, he also genuinely loves to smell other dogs' poop. All things considered, Max may not have the best taste.

Sensing weakness like a jackass smelling . . . well, just a jackass, Colin would hammer at this line of thinking: "Max needs a positive male influence. Someone to teach him how to hunt and protect loved ones and lick himself. I can do that. You, on the other hand? I know for a fact you read *Twilight. TWI. LIGHT.*"

"I read that for research! I'm a writer. I need to be in the know. I wanted to know what the fuss was."

"Then explain your Team Jacob thong. (Which looks great on you, by the way.)"

I'd hike up my jeans and change the subject: "The point is, you've spoiled him. He was a confident, normal dog before he started spending time with you. Now when I leave him alone he whines and scratches at the door. *Exactly like you.* That never happened before. Not in eight years."

"Don't act like you didn't spoil the crap out of that dog," he'd counter. "Not to mention trying to set him up with that poodle next door. Come. On. I ain't sayin' she's a gold digger . . ."

"She's a Maltese."

"I need that dog, Caprice."

And there it was. Whenever my name came out I knew it was serious, the equivalent of your parents using your first *and* middle name. And this time it wasn't because I was fifteen and got dropped home at seven a.m. by a Mötley Crüe tour bus. Um, hypothetically.

Colin hung his head. "I need to see him. You left me, which—while completely baffling to all observers—means you left me all alone. Now you're robbing me of the only affection I have. How did you become so cruel?"

"Okay," I would clarify. "Let's review the tape. You were trying to have sex with every girl you ever met that you could track down on Facebook. That is how I 'became so cruel.' Call me crazy, but that's not what I expect of the man I live with."

"Call you crazy? *Waaaaaay* ahead of you on that."

"The dog is not yours. I'm sorry, but he's not. You don't get Max as a 'thank you' for fucking me over."

"How about for fucking you."

"And there went your visitation rights."

"He's my son!"

"He was adopted by me and me alone!" I'd scream for the umpteenth time. "You're just the creepy stepfather the kids would eye warily if they existed! Your sperm didn't make Max."

"You don't know what my sperm can and can't do."

"I made damn sure of that," I'd respond, quite proud of myself. (In retrospect, our arguments didn't always make a lot of sense.)

"You're letting your own hurt feelings rob Max of something he enjoys. Max and I are buddies. Do you really want to be that petty? It causes wrinkles, you know."

"I'll think about it," I'd say, knowing full well that thinking, not being petty, causes wrinkles.

"I can't believe you left me," he'd say. Not believing, even for a second, his very own statement.

"I can't believe what you were pulling on Facebook. You were treating it like your personal dating site."

"Okay, it is possible I misunderstood their privacy settings . . . and how much slutty girls love to take pictures."

"Clearly. Seems like every single woman over thirty is using Facebook to say, 'You know that kid with the lazy eye and Gary Busey teeth I blew off in tenth grade? Maybe he wasn't so bad.'"

"God bless 'em."

Depending on the location of the jet stream that day, you could have heard my sigh of resignation along the Champs-Élysées. Definitely at the top of the Eiffel Tower. Many of these arguments ended that way. With me sighing heavily and giving in.

At first, I let myself think I was relenting because I was tired of arguing about it. But ultimately, I gave in because I knew in my heart that Max deserves extra attention. He deserves extra hours of fetch time. He deserves extra head pats and stomach rubs and sweetness and affection and TLC from anyone who wants to provide it, no matter how big a jerk that provider has been to me. And I simply can't deny Max the pleasure of a new toy every time Colin visits.

"You can have Max on Saturday," I'd say.

So, yes, it's not exactly comfortable setting up times for Max and my ex to get together. And I'm sick of putting up with the endless conversations and whining for even *more* playtime. And, yeah, I'd prefer to have nothing to do with a cheating louse of an ex-boyfriend. Ever.

But you know what? If I were a dog, I'd never hold a grudge. Or worry about one-upmanship. Or roll my eyes when a certain someone rings my doorbell with a new doggie toy. And if there's one thing I've learned from Max over the years, it's the idea of unconditional love. True, pure, unconditional love.

I guess I can put up with a little bullshit to make sure Max gets just a little bit more of the love and adoration he so freely gives to me.

Don't worry.

I still make it as miserable as possible for Colin.

Walking My Dog Through the Valley of the Shadow of Death Is a Nice Way to Start the Day

Bob Smith

Dogs are the only New Yorkers who aren't in a hurry. Schnauzers schlep, poodles prance, even manic breeds like Jack Russell terriers traipse through Manhattan. Instead of rushing everywhere and trying to piddle on four trees at once, dogs subscribe to the canine philosophy of life: Take time to stop and sniff the asses. I'm always aware that Michael and I are shirking our claims to be busy New Yorkers every time we take our dog Boswell for a walk along the Hudson.

As Michael gently leads our dog across MacDougal Street, we're both happy to give up a few hours for Bozzie. We New Yorkers have no problem wasting our own time—posting status updates about our first photography exhibition of naked clowns at a diner, inviting friends to our Monday night cabaret show built around the Minnie Riperton songbook, struggling for years to raise money for our indie film about a guy struggling for years to raise money for an indie film—but we bitterly resent *other* people wasting our time.

Though he's a beagle-basset mix, Bozzie's not superlong and low-slung like most bassets, and he's not yappy or pointy-faced like some beagles. He's barrel-chested and floppy-eared with the double sweetness of both breeds. Spending time with Bozzie is always a pleasure. He never tells stories that are dull, long, or too self-involved. He's never invited us to come see his untalented boyfriend play Fleance in *Macbeth*, and, to his credit, Bozzie has never expressed any artistic ambitions, so he's never going to put us on the spot and ask what we think of his work.

When Bozzie does become annoying, all I have to do is give him a treat. God, I wish that strategy worked at cocktail parties. The next time some writer specializing in gay Neolithic romance novels begins droning on about the hot Stonehenge sex scene in his latest self-published book, I'd promptly drop a rawhide chew stick at his feet.

Boz is a rescue dog. He was found wandering in Sullivan County and had worms, fleas, and a host of other problems, both mental and physical. The green number tattooed in his right ear made us suspect he might have been a lab dog. Boz hates all loud noise, but is particularly spooked by the sound of metal banging or scraping, which causes him to jump or shake, almost as if it brings back memories of cage doors. Bozzie has made me aware that New York's a clanging city. People are always opening or closing security gates on storefronts, stepping on the metal cellar doors on sidewalks, or throwing bottles or cans in trash bins. Even church bells terrify him.

Since Boz is prone to debilitating bouts of fear that cause him to plop down on the sidewalk shivering in terror, Michael and I always take the same route to the river, hoping that, guided by the familiar sidewalks, he'll keep his nose to the ground, tracking the comforting smells of pigeon poop, rat piss, and shit-faced NYU student vomit.

We approach an elderly woman walking a brindle-coated dachshund. A dachshund in motion always appears comical, as if the tail is wagging the dog. We stop and share forced smiles as our two dogs intimately nose each other. We're like parents on a play-date pretending not to notice their children playing doctor in front of them.

"How old is your dog?" she asks. Michael admits we don't know his exact age, but he thinks Bozzie's nine or ten. I suspect he might be a few years older. Though he's perfectly healthy and active, Bozzie's muzzle has grown whiter in the four years we've known him and gray is starting to show up in the black hair on his back. I try not to dwell on his mortality because it only makes me dwell on my own mortality. Three years ago, I was diagnosed with ALS/Lou Gehrig's disease. I'm doing well, but in order to stay well I need to keep moving, stay busy with my writing and active with my friends and family. I'm afraid if I focus on my plight, I'll end up "pulling a Bozzie" and have a meltdown on the pavement in an intersection.

On Carmine Street, Our Lady of Pompeii Roman Catholic Church reminds me of a conversation I recently had with my mother in Buffalo. "I've been praying for you. If God doesn't do this for me, I'm through with Him!" You gotta love a mom who's not afraid to write off the creator of the universe if He messes with her kid. I can't say my diagnosis has made me more spiritual. I've always had a supernatural sense of being alive, but when I contemplate any religion it only reinforces my agnosticism. First of all, I can't believe in any God who's meaner than I am—which rules out 99 percent of all faiths. I believe God should treat people as well as people treat their pets. When any religion says God has his reasons to make people suffer, I immediately think of Bozzie suffering: Would that ever be acceptable? No. Never. And it isn't acceptable with people, either. Who can ignore a dog yelping in pain? Well, God has ignored people yelping for millions of years.

The other dubious argument for God's mysterious disinterest in human pain is that He will reveal His reasons to us in the afterlife. As a writer, I can't buy that. It turns God into a hack who tags on a happy ending to every sad story. As a New Yorker, I refuse to believe in a God who's less talented than I am.

But Bozzie's also undermined my doubts about the existence of God. Often on our walks, children see Bozzie and their parents ask us if it's okay to pet him. We reassure them that Bozzie doesn't bite. He has never growled or snapped at anyone in the entire time we've known him, making him, clearly, the most pleasant New Yorker in history. Bozzie and Michael are my proof that love exists, and since science can't prove that love exists, I have to accept that there might be other unverifiable forces out there.

Happily, Bozzie's bouts of terror only occur outdoors now. When Michael first brought him home to our tiny apartment—the size of a one-bedroom doghouse—whenever I used to walk through the door, Boz would retreat to the bed in fear. Now when someone rings our buzzer, Boz runs to the door, whimpers, and then barks to be let out in the hall so he can run down the steps and greet our visitor.

His transformation from scaredy-cat to tail wagger is primarily due to Michael's relentless nutjob-bananas love for Bozzie. Michael is not a morning person, and it's my job to take Bozzie out first thing every day. I honestly don't think of taking Bozzie out before coffee as a chore. It's a preventive measure to keep Michael from becoming a grouch. But, even when Michael wakes up grumpy, he always greets Bozzie with an ecstatic, "Hello, Delicious!" Michael's joy is contagious, and every time I hear him say it, I always feel the same elation Boz feels when I toss him a biscuit. Michael can be unreasonably hard on himself in a way he never is with Bozzie or me. I wish he could treat himself like he treats Bozzie. I'd like him to look in the mirror every morning and say, "Hello, Delicious!"

At the bottom of the stairs Boz stops to look out the inner glass door. I open it, but he's too scared to move. I lean down and pet him and he gingerly steps into the entryway. I open the outer glass door, and Boz leans his head out over the threshold to look around. If someone walks by on the sidewalk, he'll duck back in. If a truck rumbles, he'll try to hide behind my legs. I usually gently scoot him with my leg onto the stoop and step around him. Once I'm outside, he musters up the courage to step down to the sidewalk. Only recently did I grasp that helping Bozzie face his day gives me the courage to face mine. I'm terrified I'll lose my ability to walk, talk, and breathe. But every morning walking Bozzie down our two flights of stairs proves that I'm okay for the day. Every time Boz lifts his leg on his favorite tinkle tree, we both feel relieved.

Bozzie treats me like an elementary school student treats a substitute teacher. He can be bad and act out because he knows I lack Michael's authority. On the days when Michael's out and I stay home and write in our apartment, Bozzie feels free to poop in the kitchen in the morning. As I pick up the poop and spray the floor, I yell at him, "Bozzie Bad Boy!" and I mean it. Boz will bow his head and retreat to the bedroom, looking dejected—his jowls drooping like sad sacks filled with tears—and sit and wait until I cave in and come and rub his belly.

Later in the afternoon, he barks in the living room for a dog biscuit. He never barks for biscuits with Michael. I know I sound like every crazy dog owner handing out a Mensa membership to his Fido, but I truly believe Bozzie understands that I turn into a biscuit soft touch if he makes me laugh. He definitely puts on a performance. I'll be typing on my laptop on the couch, and Boz will come stand near me and go into the downward-facing dog yoga position, emitting a low grumble. I try to pretend not to notice how adorable he is, but then he'll whimper, and my heart overrides my head, and I instinctively turn to address his distress. Once eye contact is established, he'll stare for a moment and then bark. Barking is actually a new skill for Bozzie, as he had only barked about once a year for the first two years we had him. I'll say, "No," but once I laugh—and he always makes me laugh—I get up and Bozzie races me to the kitchen.

Michael and I are usually attempting to do fifteen things at once, so on our walks we follow Bozzie's lead and try to find seven years of pleasure in each New York minute. Michael's a screenwriter and a playwright who's currently working on a musical scheduled to open Off Broadway. He's written and sold two screenplays in the past year, and he also teaches screenwriting at NYU. I'm always working on a new novel, running out to help stand-up pals write jokes for their acts, or helping other friends punch up the acts of big Las Vegas stars. I also teach a comic-essay writing class at NYU. And Michael and I have a play ethic that's as overdeveloped as our work ethic. We try to see well-reviewed films, plays, and art exhibitions, read important books, and spend time talking about all of them with our friends.

Bozzie likes our friends almost as much as we do. He adores our neighbors Michael and Susan. Susan is Bozzie's best friend, and anytime I open our door he runs to her door and cocks his head and stands motionless, listening. If Boz hears her speaking, he whimpers, barks, and literally tries to dig his way through the door. Next up is our friend Eddie, who once cared for Boz when we were in London. When he sees Eddie on the stairs, Boz goes berserk, and I suspect that Eddie must be an even bigger biscuit pushover than I am. Then there's Jaffe, Michael's screenwriting partner. Jaffe is one of those small-dog-carrying gay men. Jaffe's also cared for Boz, and since Jaffe is so besotted by his dog, we've always felt confident he'll also spoil our dog. It's easy to mock a gay man who carries his dog like a purse, but people misunderstand the relationship. Buster isn't Jaffe's accessory; it's the other way around, and Jaffe knows and relishes it.

Turning right on Seventh Avenue, we cut down Leroy Street, a lovely strip of Greenwich Village shaded by large ginkgo trees. There's a pool, library, and park on one side and a row of brownstones on the other. A commemorative plaque on the library says the poet Marianne Moore wrote there. I'm guessing only a handful of people have read the plaque since its installation. The minuscule, hard-to-read inscription and bronze patina make it indistinguishable from the brickwork. Michael pointed out, as a memorial, it seems designed to keep Marianne Moore obscure.

We're especially observant on Leroy. Michael heard Arthur Laurents supposedly lives on the block. So far we've not seen the famously opinionated writer and theater director, but I like to think someday our wish will be fulfilled, and he'll condemn or congratulate us for letting Bozzie pee in front of his house. Either would thrill Michael and me, but Bozzie would likely give him a cursory sniff, as he's only impressed by celebrities bearing biscuits.

We always pick up coffee at a restaurant on the corner of Hudson and grab an empty coffee cup for Bozzie's water. As we approach the West Side Highway, Bozzie walks faster. He loves the river.

Across the highway, we sit on the park benches facing the water, sipping our coffees as I comment on the passing joggers.

"He's hot! I love the way his bicep looks like it's testing the tensile strength of his Celtic tattoo."

"Wow! He's got guts—literally and figuratively—to be jogging shirtless."

"Hmmm. Why would someone jog pushing a stroller? Isn't that teaching your kid to be a layabout?"

My judgments, though borderline catty, are only designed to make Michael laugh, and my tone is never harsh, as it's impossible to forget, while they exercise, I'm the bench potato.

We don't sit for long, quickly losing interest in watching New Yorkers using their leisure time to run. It's like fish making an effort to swim three times a week. We walk out onto the pier—a plank of park jutting into the river. It has trees and a lawn, benches and tables, and architecturally designed canopies offering shade. On summer days, the pier feels like New York's gay backyard, filled with shirtless hotties tanning on the grass. For me, it always evokes the Janus-like sensation of being a middle-aged gay man. One face looks back and remembers my strong jaw and tight body, while the other face looks forward to a double chin and the love handles that dare not speak their name. Despite my generosity with the biscuits, in the four years Bozzie's lived with us, he's lost weight and looks fit, and I like to think he holds his head high as he parades past the buff-eteria.

We take a different route back to our apartment, but to make the trip easier on Bozzie, it's always the same different route. We cut down Barrow Street and cross Hudson and enter my favorite block in the Village. Commerce Street curves into Barrow, and at the junction of the two are a pair of matching town houses with mansard roofs separated by a yard. They're my favorite houses in Manhattan, and I want to live in one of them.

I once said to Michael, "If I had a billion dollars, I'd buy both these houses. We'd live in one and the other would be for visiting friends."

Michael looked at me as if I were an idiot. "No," he said. "You'd live in one. I'd live in the other."

This was a comment on my housekeeping.

Michael's nickname for me is Slobola, which to my ear sounds like the surname of an obscure depressing Romanian writer that Susan Sontag once championed and whom I dutifully read and hated in college. Though Michael is an unabashed animal lover, he hates dust bunnies. He vacuums them up with the ruthlessness of a fur-greedy brute clubbing seal pups, and he's unamused when I suggest he should regard them affectionately as Bozzie's hair puppies. Michael's right, of course. I am the messy one. He's pointed out that I'd never leave a scrap of litter in the millions of acres of wilderness of my beloved Alaska, but I'll happily live amid a temperate rain forest of papers in our apartment. Michael is a pessimist and sees our apartment as half dirty, while I always see it as half clean. Every time I leave a pair of black socks on the floor and Michael picks them up, I feel as guilty as Bozzie after he's pooped in the kitchen. If only Michael would yell, "Bad Bob! Bad!" and then a half hour later come in and pet me.

On our return, when we turn down Bleecker, Bozzie picks up the pace. He knows we're close to home. In fact, he will pull against Michael if he tries to take a different route. Our walks always make me feel how blessed I am to have both Michael and Bozzie in my life. (If an agnostic can, indeed, feel blessed. When someone sneezes I say, "Bless you!" and repress the urge to add, "although I have strong doubts someone or something blesses any of us.") Michael has been unshakably supportive, humorous, and patient about my illness, without ever letting me forget: coffee grounds left in the sink, not so supportive.

A dog's year is a long time for someone with Lou Gehrig's disease, and there have been moments of anguish since my diagnosis. My doctor wanted to put me on an antidepressant immediately, but I haven't felt depressed. I actually spend most days feeling happy. My contentment has astounded my friends, all of whom are on antidepressants. It's got to be rough for them. Who wouldn't be bummed out if a guy whose prognosis is three to five years is almost always in a better mood than you?

Bozzie and Michael have made me realize I've always led a dog's life. I'm messy and, according to Michael, leave my hair everywhere in the bathroom. I like a routine. I'm content to eat the same meals day in and day out for years at a time. (Right now, my lunch for the past eight months has been an Otto Goodness turkey sandwich and smoky tomato soup from Murray's cheese shop on Bleecker. The staff—Nina, Sydney, and Catherine—always say, "Hi, Bob. The usual?" which always makes my tail wag.) I'm intensely loyal to my friends and family. (I growl fiercely when my loved ones are threatened. When a friend received one lone bad review of his otherwise highly praised book on Goodreads, I became enraged and posted a scathing review of his critic's poor grammar.) I'm with dogs in ignoring all threats of damnation and never feeling guilty about having fun. If Bozzie wants to same-sex sniff another dog, he doesn't worry about some bigoted desert hick named Leviticus. (Many religions believe dogs don't have souls and won't make it to heaven. That reason alone would make me give those faiths the heave-ho.)

Like a dog, I don't have any doubts about what I'm doing with my life. Ever since I was sixteen, if I write every morning and think of something clever or funny, it makes me happy. I'm content if Michael lets me hump his leg once a week, and if you bring me a lime cornmeal cookie from Amy's Bread, I'll be your friend for life.

There has been one significant change in my personality since I began measuring my life in dog years. I no longer have any time or patience for mean-spirited idiots. If you profess support for Republicans, have doubts about global warming, show eagerness to drill in the Arctic National Wildlife Refuge, defend torture and marriage inequality, or oppose universal health care in my presence, you'll quickly discover that, unlike Bozzie, I bite.

It's not like dogs don't have fears. A dropped fork rattles Bozzie, and I'm afraid of dying horribly. But Bozzie doesn't let his fears rule him, and neither do I. Bozzie is proof that nightmares aren't always a life sentence. I remember when AIDS meant death and communism would last forever but, like a dog, I don't know what's going to happen. I've always possessed Bozzie's hard-earned optimism. It's nose-to-the-ground practical and not at all sentimental.

You won't get a treat every time you want one, but what's wrong with going through life believing you might get a biscuit?

A Courtly Soul

Rita Mae Brown

A gentleman makes a woman feel like a lady.

Even though most of us aren't bombshells, the little attentions bestowed upon us make us feel that we are.

A gesture as simple as standing when a lady enters the room flatters us. Being a Virginian, I am especially susceptible to such behavior. In fact, I crave it.

Idler always stood when I walked into the kennels. He'd walk on my outside if we stepped out. He'd wait for me to motion for him to jump into the truck first. Later, in retirement, when he moved up to the house, he never failed to rise when I blasted through the door.

Impeccable manners.

A big, tricolor American foxhound, he was a gentle soul, so industrious his name didn't fit him. Not pushy, he watched over me. If he thought another hound acted rudely, he'd bare his teeth. What woman can resist such protectiveness?

Idler came to me in 1994 from the late Mrs. Paul Summers, Jr., MFH, of Farmington Hunt Club in Charlottesville, Virginia.

Jill and I both revered Bywaters blood, a special type of foxhound bred before the War Between the States for the difficult soil conditions of Virginia. After the late Unpleasantness Between the States, this special line was refined, raised to new heights by a veteran of the war, last name Bywaters. The blood existed before, but now it had a name, and the succeeding generations of Bywaters, all fabulous hound men, carried forth the torch.

I hasten to add that American foxhunters *chase*, we don't *kill*.

The Bywaters blood fell out of fashion in the sixties, and by the seventies a few special masters preserved it, Jill Summers, a genius at breeding and I mean genius, being one. Hounds and horses, like hemlines, are the victims of fashion.

When I revived Oak Ridge Hunt in Nelson County, Jill generously gave me six couple of hounds, Bywaters blood. Hounds have been measured in twos, couples, since the pharaohs. Consistency has its virtues. So, I had twelve hounds, six couple, and very good hounds they were, Idler being one.

I built a temporary kennel dubbed the Taj Mahal. The best I can say for my skills is it kept them warm and kept the rain out. But Idler enjoyed it because, having no running water, I carried it out of the north branch of the Rockfish River in buckets. Twenty-two degrees Fahrenheit the river ran once you waded beyond the ice parts, so there was always water, but I turned blue. Idler accompanied me. Sweet fellow, if I stepped into the water, he stepped in with me.

He liked to watch the smallmouth bass (rockfish), the minnows, crappies, and crayfish. Once I had a proper kennel constructed with the help of the late Jack Eicher, a professional huntsman, Idler liked his new quarters. They all did, but Idler still wanted to go down to the river. Every day, we'd take our walk. No leash. Just the two of us. He noticed squirrels, hawks, the direction of the wind. As I pay great attention to these things, we had a lot to discuss. But with his fabulous nose, he could smell weather coming in half a day before I knew it. If he returned to his sleeping space, made a burrow in the straw, I knew when I reached the house to turn up the heat.

Tidy, clean, Idler never ripped up a thing. He greeted every guest to the kennels, willingly showing them his quarters. If you brought a cookie to reward him for the tour, he was blissfully happy.

He was six when he came to me, in great shape, had earned his Ph.D. in hunting, too. The other hounds deferred to him. I learned to defer to him as well.

Idler taught me with exquisite patience.

Growing up with a great-uncle who was a kennelman at Green Spring Valley Hunt Club, a grandfather who hunted his own small pack on foot, and men and women who adored hunting on horseback, on foot, with hounds, with gundogs, I thought I was well educated. He forgave me my misconception.

My grandfather, PopPop Harmon, not a talker, did preach to me: Trust your hounds. If you don't trust them, don't hunt them. I trusted Idler. His senses, much keener than I can imagine, picked up scent, changes in the temperature and humidity, before I did. When you're hunting a fox, an animal who can process information at warp speed, you need to pay attention. Every second counts, really. And Idler, great though he was, couldn't think as fast as a fox, but he had drive, unbelievable drive, and once he found the scent he was on.

He taught me to trust him in the field the first day of cubbing, the first year Oak Ridge was reborn. Our territory, rough, tried the patience of all the giving saints. It takes years to properly open territory in this part of the world, clear trails, build jumps, find fords. Out I rode, cast the pack on a high rise. Cubbing, the beginning of hunting, starts in Virginia in early September. Oak Ridge goes out at seven thirty a.m. The heat comes on fast, and you're finished by nine or nine thirty a.m. Scent has evaporated. I cast on the west side, for the sun had yet to kiss those pastures. However, a breeze blew in from the northwest. The pack dutifully began to work.

Nothing.

Idler came up to me, stood, opened his mouth for one deep yowl.

I said, "Get 'em up."

Now, the hounds and the horses know the verbal commands and the horn calls, for foxhunting is a musical sport. On a good day for sound that horn call can carry over a mile.

Idler heard the command and saved my bacon. He didn't disobey me. I said, "Get 'em up." He crossed the farm road, dipped down to a little stream, the pack followed him.

Sitting on the now retired Toma, I had a moment because that wasn't what I intended. Before I could call them back, Idler opened his mouth, his basso profundo voice sending shivers right up my spine and everyone else's, too. Then the whole pack sang in chorus. I hung on.

He knew where there was a chance for scent. He didn't disobey me, but when I opened the door he took his own line and we had a lovely day. That was when I realized truly what PopPop meant when he said, "Trust your hounds."

If scent had vanished and someone had an involuntary dismount, Idler, if in the vicinity, would trot over to offer solace. If scent was hot, he'd give the human a sideways glance but kept on.

All the years I'd hunted in the field and loved it hadn't taught me a thing about being the huntsman. Thanks to Idler, I was on the fast track with recalled wisdom from PopPop and Jack, both of whom I still miss terribly. If the horn is in your hand, the hunt is, too. Thank God for Idler in those early years.

A powerfully built fellow, he weighed eighty pounds. Foxhounds run between fifty-five and eighty pounds. There's always variation, but that's the basic range. Ideally, one would like a pack the same size and the same weight. It can take decades to breed that and many never do. However, what really matters is can they hunt, the hell with how they look.

Idler had a strong face, large expressive eyes, and bowlegs. Running, you didn't notice. Walking, he resembled a sailor deep into the rum. Sometimes you had to laugh, but he always forgave you.

The years rolled by. I'd learned his lessons: Get on terms with your fox quickly; if it's a middling day swing into that wind every chance you get; watch my tail first. Not once did he call me too dumb to have been born, but he must have thought it.

The season came when he couldn't stay up front, then a later season he fell to the middle and finally behind. He hated being behind, and I knew it was time to retire him.

Up to the house he came. When I opened the door and told him, "Kennel up!" there, in his path, was a gray cat, Pewter, who would never have that high school senior superlative "Best Personality."

In short, she was a hateful bitch.

She lived with house dogs and bludgeoned them daily. Idler listened to her abuse, refused to reply, and walked by her. She then followed, screaming obscenities. The other dogs ran for cover. He walked into the living room, spied the sofa, and jumped up. She jumped on the back to lean over and continue acting in a non-Christian manner. I petted him, and he went to sleep.

After a week, Pewter and Idler were the odd couple. She even rode in the truck with him, curling up on his back or in his front legs. Maybe this isn't on par with the miracle of the loaves and the fishes, but it certainly impressed me.

His perfect manners transformed my harpy into, well, a pussycat. Now it was the three of us who went everywhere together. What a sight we must have been, "a seventh seal" minus all the humans but one.

You know, he always rose when I entered a room.

By the time he was fourteen, he had to take medications for aching joints. Long walks became short walks. Pewter would minister to him when we'd come back to the house. He'd drink water, flop down, and she'd lick his face then purr as she curled up, two souls content in one another's company.

One day, I came home and he struggled to rise.

Always the gentleman; I knew his time had come.

The vet made a house call, and he passed away quietly with Pewter and me by his side. It's good to be with an animal or human when they cross over. At least, I think it is.

Poor Pewter mourned her friend for months. She finally revived. She no longer attacked the other dogs, but she never selected one as a special friend. He'd worked his magic on her as he had with me.

I owe that hound so much, but most of all I still always smile because he knew how to take care of a lady.

The Little Rascal

Beth Harbison

He was as black as coal. His eyes were soulful pools of shadow and light, promising love, devotion, loyalty, but a little hint of trouble. Classic Bad Boy stuff. His smile was so white, it was as if it was luminous. He was strong, built almost entirely of muscle and bone, and created an impression of danger with every powerful movement.

At two feet four inches, his physique was undeniably slight, but what he lacked in height he made up for in energy.

His name was Rascal.

He was a one-year-old black Lab.

In the year before we met him, my family had lost both our beloved golden retriever–Lab mixes, Zuzu and Bailey, at the ripe old ages of fourteen and fifteen. Zuzu had gone first, even though she was the younger one. I'd always had a special place in my heart for her: since the moment I'd brought my infant son home from the hospital, she had slept every night by his crib. Her devotion was so clear that we began to refer to her as Auntie Zuzu, the name our son had come to know her by, occasionally to the surprise and confusion of guests.

We had gotten Bailey when our daughter had started kinder-garten, and she died two weeks before that little girl went off to college for the first time. The melancholy was enormous.

Over the years, I had looked for the breeder we had gotten Bailey and Zuzu from, to refer her to friends, but never with any luck. After Bailey died, I saw an ad for the golden-Lab mixes a few towns over from ours and, by a stroke of luck, it was the same breeder (she just had a new name and new farm). We were thrilled, and we rushed out and got two new puppies for way too much money because we were so excited to have dogs from the same bloodlines.

And they're wonderful dogs. They love us, and they love each other. Yes, perhaps they are a *little* cliquish (my sister calls them "the blondes," with more than a little snark, because her desperate little dog bounces around them like a superball that flies out of bounds in a game of jacks, and, still, they never pay any attention to him). But they are good dogs.

However, before we'd found the breeder and decided to go that route, I'd vowed that any and every dog I got subsequently would be a rescue. So I worried that buying the blondes gave me bad dog juju. And of course, after we had them, adding a rescue would have been unfair to all three, so what we decided to do was foster. We could still help, but it wouldn't be a long-term commit-ment on our part that might upset the canine balance in our house. A few weeks caring for a dog that would otherwise have ended up euthanized in a kill shelter was *nothing*! Why, we prob-ably wouldn't even notice a difference!

Enter Rascal.

He came from a kill shelter in North Carolina. His family had inexplicably given him up, even knowing what his fate would be.

How does anyone get a puppy, raise him for an entire year, see how he loves them and depends on them, then just give him up to a cold, impersonal prison filled with other frightened and doomed animals? The selfishness that goes into that decision is completely beyond my comprehension. The fact that he was a beautiful, healthy, black English Lab—a breed that is constantly in demand and quite costly—just makes it even more puzzling why they didn't choose one of many other simple options in order to find him a family.

But they didn't. And as a result, I was the last leg of his long relay from North Carolina to Maryland. I met the older gentleman who drove the second-to-last leg of the relay in the parking lot of a California Pizza Kitchen about thirty miles south of my home.

As soon as I walked up to the black Mercedes, I saw a shadow inside start bouncing around, white teeth flashing with joy at seeing *another human*. I opened the door and loved him instantly—his optimism was startling. Bless his heart, he didn't know what he'd been through and that he shouldn't trust us all so openly. He was just ready to love anyone.

We did the handoff, and Rascal sat on my lap quietly all the way home.

Apparently, he's a fan of the car. Like babies who fall asleep in the car seat, he was lulled to sleep by the drive, and I was lulled into a sense of complacency with him. He was an angel! Just a quiet, sweet boy in need of love! Maybe, somehow, we could even keep him. . . .

I didn't realize his particular level of energy until we got home.

I had understood that he'd been neutered the day before and, having had only female dogs in the past for whom the equivalent operation is major, I believed he would need some TLC for a few days. Perhaps he'd lie quietly on a blanket while I brought him shallow bowls of homemade chicken noodle soup. We'd sit before the fireplace, him dozing and me content with the knowledge that I was a crucial link in the chain of his life.

I love dogs, his well-being was of the utmost importance to me, but doing a favor—no matter *what* the favor—never comes without at least a little bit of self-satisfied smugness on my part. It's one of the darker, more shameful parts of my character. Yes, I wanted to save this dog, I wanted to help at all costs, but I also wanted to be viewed as kind of an angel of mercy, if only by him.

Anyway, my visions of tenderly nursing him back to life and happiness were shattered immediately, along with two flowerpots on my porch, when I opened the car door and he shot out like a bullet, flying up the steps to the front door and flailing around, sniffing wildly at everything in front of him, knocking over everything behind him, and depositing a good amount of viscous saliva onto the wood decking, onto the house siding, and onto the clothes of everyone who was trying to catch him in order to calm him down and take him inside.

That's when I made my first call to the PetConnect coordinator, Mary.

"I think there's been a mistake," I explained. "I thought Rascal was supposed to be neutered yesterday, but it seems like he wasn't."

"What do you mean?"

"Well, he's very . . . energetic." And I'll confess that, for a moment, I was really hoping there *had* been a mistake and that there was still hope for that quiet Florence Nightingale scene I had envisioned.

There was a pause, during which I'm pretty sure she was thinking maybe she should have checked me out more thoroughly.

"When male dogs get fixed they don't have the downtime female dogs have," she explained.

This was news to me.

Bad news.

"Ah, well!" I responded, my voice an octave higher than when I'd begun the conversation. "Just wanted to make sure that . . . he . . . was handling the surgery properly." I ended the conversation in a flurry of words as I watched a black figure dive in and then out of my view out the back window.

For the rest of the day, Rascal bounded around outside, charming the blondes into all kinds of destruction. A plush dog pillow from Costco was reduced to cotton candy within the first hour; stuffed animals were stolen from my son's room and systematically dismantled all over the house, a button eye here, a shredded red shirt reading "Pooh" there; our once quiet yard was suddenly the "twilight bark" soundtrack from *101 Dalmatians*; charcoal briquettes were somehow removed from the Rubbermaid bin we kept them in and scattered all around, many half consumed; all of the dogs hurled themselves repeatedly against the glass door panes, in an effort to get in and inflict their play on the hardwood floors, the noise issuing from their twelve long-nailed paws sounding akin to pouring a one-pound bag of Skittles from the ceiling.

Within a few hours, Rascal had gone from being a pitiable, gentle creature to being a pair of wild eyes behind a snarf-smeared door window as we huddled inside, wondering, in silent camaraderie, what on earth we were going to do and how we were going to do it before our house was destroyed.

We *had* to get him adopted.

First thing I needed to do was get a decent picture of him. The one I'd seen on the Web site was a little too mug-shot-ish. Too much whites of the eyes, not enough warmth.

It was the kind of picture that, if taken of a human and posted on Match.com, would have pegged him immediately as a psychopathic killer. And, no, people would not be looking at him with an eye toward dating (please, God), but in a society where we are so conditioned to look at people, products, houses, and so on with an eye toward acquiring or not acquiring, I thought he needed to look more *accessible*.

And, honestly, more like *himself*. Because he was a very cute dog, apart from the moments of sheer insanity.

So I tried to make him sit on the porch so I could take a picture. The moment I took a step backward, just far enough so I could get more than his left nostril in the frame, he went wild, leaping at me as if I'd just tagged him in a game of *ghost in the graveyard*.

In my best alpha dog voice, I yelled, "No!"

It was a command he found hilarious.

I tried to channel Barbara Woodhouse, the British dog expert and disciplinary hard-ass, and the original—and best—dog whisperer, as far as I'm concerned.

"No!" I grabbed his collar and held him steady, as originally instructed on *Training Dogs the Woodhouse Way*. Her contention was that any dog could be trained in six minutes with loving firmness.

Sixty firm minutes—and about six hundred blurry pictures of some vague in-motion part of his body—later, I was ready to give up.

Then Rascal lay down, his back legs flat and froggy, in what I took to be a sign of trusting relaxation, and his chin between his front paws, and he looked at me. Adoring. Agreeable. Grateful.

Imploring. Or so I imagined.

He just wanted a home, a family to love him. A place where he could learn the ropes one time and stay there. It was as if he knew he was a boarder here, living in a way station on his way to . . . somewhere. Neither of us knew where that would be.

Why learn *my* rules when learning the last person's rules had led him to a rural animal shelter without the patience or resources to let him live, and when the next person's rules might be different from mine and end up counterproductive in the same way?

"You're right, buddy." I sat down on the steps in front of him and put my hand on his head.

He rolled onto his side, cupped his paws around my wrist, and lapped sloppily at my hand.

He *wanted* to love and be loved.

But I guess that meant being loved for who he was and not who I tried, during my very brief time with him, to make him.

I scratched his ears for a few minutes in silence, his fur attached mohair-mitten-like to my saliva-covered hand, then got up to go inside. He sat up, but not all the way.

He was still. And quiet.

And that's when I got the picture.

I uploaded it to my contact at PetConnect, and they put it on his little Love Me profile page.

The next day he had a potential taker.

She was a frail woman, bones like a bird, and *cat person* was written all over her face.

"There have been break-ins in my neighborhood," she told me. "I want to get a dog that will look intimidating."

I was torn. I didn't think that was a good reason to adopt a dog—it sounded like exactly the reason that would be cited later when she wanted to get rid of him. On the other hand, he needed a home.

He *really needed a home.*

So I introduced them. I needn't have worried about the moral quandary of whether or not I should encourage the adoption—she hated him on sight.

I'd like to say the feeling was clearly mutual, but he was as friendly to her as he was to everyone. It was heartbreaking.

The young, newly married couple that came the next day wasn't much better. Though she talked about having grown up with dogs, having had them all her life, the fact that she was wearing D&G gladiators that I could already imagine shredded into a mess of high-end leather spaghetti and a Cynthia Ashby slip dress I could picture being pulled on from behind told me that she was much more of a cockapoo person. Sure enough, when Rascal jumped up at her, she pushed feebly at him with manicured hands, and her husband looked on helplessly, clearly trying to keep his own Polo-wear clean.

I loved that they wanted to adopt a rescue. I was just sorry that they were so ill prepared to do so.

Three long days later, someone new had seen something in Rascal's picture and called to make an appointment to come meet him.

She was a vet tech, a woman with two young sons and a lot of land, and she was very interested in meeting Rascal.

I thought—briefly—that I had a great idea.

"Can I reasonably give him Benadryl?" I asked Mary.

"I'm sorry?"

"To make him tired."

There was a pause. "What do you mean?"

"Well, you know how you can give your kids Benadryl to help them . . ."

Even as I spoke, I realized this wasn't sounding right.

". . . Umm, *sleep* when they're up every night until after midnight, swinging like Tarzan on the drapes, and shrieking like crazed Philadelphia Eagles fans?"

"You *drug* your *kids*?"

At this point, she is no longer just thinking *she* should have checked me out more thoroughly, but possibly that child protective services should as well.

"No, of course not! I just meant . . . remember the old *SNL* thing with Puppy Uppers and Doggy Downers? It was just a joke."

And I rambled until I hoped I had obscured things enough to make her think *she* was wrong in what she thought I said, and not that *I* was wrong to say it.

Now, in my defense, we *did* have a dog once that would get so freaked out on the Fourth of July that the vet told us to slip her a Benadryl before the fireworks began so that she would be a little drowsy and thus not get so scared. But after the reaction from the woman with the rescue mission, I wasn't a hundred percent sure my vet was on the up and up.

So we flew solo, didn't drug Rascal, and basically prayed he'd behave like the nice young man we knew he could be when his latest prospective parent came to look at him.

She came; he was wild and enthusiastic and over-the-top and we sighed, certain in the knowledge that this, too, had failed. And it was a real shame because *this one* seemed so nice!

But she fell in love with him! She got down on the floor with him and played with him like she'd known him since puppyhood! She *got* that he was a Lab that had a certain, fairly predictable, level of energy.

She was *okay* with that!

Step one was completed. She was interested. She was filling out the application to adopt him, pending approval of her family. Two days later she came back with her children and he was even *more* wild, *more* enthusiastic, and *more* over-the-top, and *they* fell in love.

It was a match made in heaven!

Of course the adoption went through without a hitch: She was a perfect candidate, she had room, she had children, she had realistic expectations, and she had *desire* to adopt Rascal.

I've seldom seen anything as beautiful as the excitement on the children's faces as they pulled up to our house in a van already equipped with a crate, bags of food, and "twelve toys!" they'd just picked out at PetSmart. They packed him up and took him to his new home. I watched from the front porch as he eagerly jumped into their car, as comfortable with them as if he'd been with them always. Not a trace of fear or the mistrust his past might have suggested he should have.

Just love.

I went back in the house and sat down. It was quiet. The blondes, without their goading companion, had returned to their more docile state of lying in the sun and thumping their tails on the deck when they sensed eye contact.

Life was normal again.

And a little . . . emptier.

And it was funny because I really thought I'd be a lot more relieved when he had left because the difference between two dogs and three was like the difference between a firefly and fire. I went outside with the blondes, and they lay down on the porch for a nap, elbows hitting the wood in that familiar sound I'd been longing to hear for weeks, instead of the sounds of moist panting and nails screaming across the hardwood floors followed by the crash of something heavy and the frantic scurrying of the guilty parties.

All in all, though, it was good to have life back to normal. And it was good to feel like we'd helped this soul, though there was always a question in the back of our minds as to how things had worked out. Yes, his new family seemed perfect, every instinct I had told me they were perfect, but how many times as a teenager had I tried to make deals with God to let me have the guy who seemed perfect, only to find later he was creepy/annoying/disappointing in ways I never could have predicted? What if this was one of those situations, where I had been so eager for the outcome I wanted that I'd missed important clues or even warnings that this was an ill-fated match?

Was Rascal okay, or had I taken him from one unfortunate situation and put him, trusting, right into another one?

The answer came six months later.

It was the holiday season, a time when we hug our own a little closer to us, even while our hearts go out to those with no one and nothing. I'm always a little melancholy during the holidays, thinking about the year that's passed and wondering if I did anything that was truly worth my salt. But this time the question was answered by a trip to the mailbox: Rascal's new family had sent one of those photo Christmas cards with a message of goodwill embossed over a picture of the whole family . . . including Rascal.

He was the one in the Santa hat!

Are You a Rascal or a Ringo?

Jeff Marx

If you're ever tending a shop, or waiting tables in a restaurant, or working the customer service counter at an airline, or even just standing in line to get into a Wade Rouse book reading, and you happen to overhear two gay guys snickering as they pass you, nudging each other and pointing, laughing and whispering, *"That was a Rascal!"* or *"That was a Ringo!"* let me explain what we mean by it.

My boyfriend and I have started dividing the world into *Rascals* and *Ringos*, based on the two very distinct personalities of our dogs. It's not nice, but it helps us better describe (and perhaps understand, by making sweeping generalizations) some of the people we meet. And probably more important, it helps us to accept and normalize the behavior of our animal companions, which is an ongoing challenge.

We have two rescue dogs, Rascal and Ringo. They're brothers, although we're fairly sure they have different fathers.

By the way, did you know that dogs from the same litter can have different fathers? We once shared this strange fact of nature with a close friend's sister, who was at our house for dinner. She had a grand old time laughing at us and in a condescending tone explaining that she was *an animal husbandry major* in college, and that puppies from the same litter having two different fathers was the stupidest thing she'd ever heard. "That's *not* how it works," she told us. Didn't we understand basic biology? We weren't all that invested in the concept; it was just something we heard somewhere, so we figured we must have heard it wrong. Certainly, Ms. Animal Husbandry would know. . . . But when she left, we Googled it, and sure enough, dogs in the same litter *can* have different fathers! She must have skipped class that day. I never got to say, "I told you so!" So I hope she's reading this essay. I'll be watching my Facebook wall for an apology.

Anyway, our Rascally-Boy and our Ringo-Dingo are a great illustration of the old nature versus nurture question: How much of a dog's personality is predetermined, and how much does the environment in which the animal was raised shape its personality? This is actually playing a role in helping us decide how to have a baby—through adoption or the grow-your-own (surrogacy) route. On the one hand, we adopted these dogs and couldn't love them more. We're not biologically related to them, but we couldn't imagine our lives without them. On the other hand, if we had been asked to list the qualities we wanted in a dog, and had any control over it, Ringo isn't exactly the one we would have chosen. Rascal is.

Even though Rascal and Ringo may have had different fathers, they certainly had the same mother, so at least half of their genes come from the same source. They're both little black terriers, twenty-five to thirty pounds. Rascal is handsome and winsome, with white patches in just the right places, brown highlights under his nose, and beautiful, adorable, expressive brown eyebrows; he's extremely handsome, and he knows it. He reminds us of Jake Gyllenhaal running down the beach in board shorts. Ringo, on the other hand, is scraggly and scrawny, with a white ring around his nose, and always looks like he just rolled out of bed without showering and/or got hit by lightning. He's a bit of a cross between Kramer from *Seinfeld,* Jim from *Taxi*, and Grover from *Sesame Street.*

We got them at the same time and we've brought them up in the same way since the age of six weeks. However, Rascal and Ringo couldn't be more different in temperament and constitution. Either they were born this way or they have taken very different meanings from the same well-intentioned lessons we provided them.

Rascal is charming and gregarious and loving and cautious, but ultimately brave and wonderful and sweet. He will bark at a guest who comes over for dinner upon their arrival, but by the end of the night he's curled up next to them.

Ringo is sweet, too, but "special." He cowers and shakes and scrambles away from strangers and barks at every noise he hears and refuses to make eye contact when he's not comfortable—which is often.

When there's incessant barking for no reason and one of the Daddys is about to yell "Unnecessary noise prohibited!" or get out the spray bottle, the culprit is usually Ringo. We know this because Rascal purposefully comes over to find us and quietly demonstrate that it's not him. See, what a smart dog!

Rascal is overweight (because he has two dinners every night—his and Ringo's), and he answers to the nickname "Fatty."

Ringo is skinny (because he doesn't always eat his dinner before his brother gets to it), and timid, and doesn't usually answer at all when we call him. We suspect that he knows we want him to come, but he's usually too caught up in his own neurosis to respond.

And so, for us, *a Rascal* is anyone who appears to us (upon first glance) to be fat, playful, self-confident, bossy, or generally well-adjusted. *A Ringo*, on the other hand, is anyone we think may be too skinny, scared, stubborn, anxious, or stupid.

Are you a Rascal or a Ringo?

Rascal is always the first one up on our bed at night; he pushes his brother out of the way when he wants something. When we're not paying attention to him, he'll harrumph at us or paw at us, or pull our wrists away from the laptop, until we give in and cuddle him.

Ringo is scared of his own shadow and it took forever to teach him to follow his brother's good example and walk through the plastic-flap doggie door. The sound of the flap closing scares him, so he'd rather hold it in than jump through.

When we were potty training the dogs, we would keep them in a crate like we were told to, so they'd build up a good reserve of pee and poo, and then we'd let them outside and praise them generously for peeing and pooing on the grass. Then we'd let them back in the house for some good loving.

Rascal picked it up fast. After about a week, he'd let himself out through the doggie door, and do his business, just to earn our praise, which he loved. If we'd forgotten to leave the doggie door unlocked for some reason, Rascal would bark at us to let us know he needed to go out. He's such a good boy!

Ringo didn't quite get it. It took him forever to learn the rules. There was one time we were out on the grass, waiting for the dogs to do their thing so we could praise them and give them positive reinforcement. Rascal did it, and Ringo peed only a little. But we heaped praise on them and brought them both into the house, up on the bed.

It was then that Ringo looked at me, to make sure I was watching, and pissed right on the bed. I guess he thought the praise was for peeing in general, not for peeing on the grass.

I yelled "Noooooooo!" and swooped him up and brought him outside to do it on the grass (which he didn't). WTF. We potty trained them in the same way but one picked it up and one still hasn't! To this day, Ringo still poops *next to* the grass instead of on it.

Rascal is pretty much a dream dog. All of our friends and family agree. Why can't Ringo be the same? Life would be so much easier.

It's embarrassing when people bend down to pet Ringo, and he cowers and shakes and snarls. I'm sure people think we abuse him. We tell them he's a "rescue dog," and everyone compassionately nods knowingly. "Poor thing, he must have gone through something terrible." We're careful to omit the fact that we've had him for over three years and he's gotten worse over time. We're constantly making excuses for him and apologizing for his rude behavior.

In fact, often rather than apologize, we lie. When we're walking the dogs and another dog approaches, and the owner asks if they're friendly, we say, "Oh, yes, they're totally friendly."

We know Ringo is ornery, but we hope that by socializing him with other dogs, he'll learn to be nicer. Of course, this invariably ends with him snarling and snapping at the other dog, and we say, "Oh, my goodness! He's never done that before!"

Yes, we're *those* people. Watch out for us on your next walk.

We hate it when people tell us that their dogs are friendly when they're actually not, but even more so, we hate admitting to strangers that we have a baby with emotional and behavioral problems. Don't get me wrong, we love this dog to death, we don't know what we'd do without him, and we can't imagine what our lives would be like if we had chosen another dog from the litter instead of him. He's our special little guy—our Ringo-Dingo, our Sweet Little Dingo Bear, our Dingle Jingle von Tingle. At night, when the house is quiet and it's just the Daddys and the doggies, Ringo is such a lover. He cuddles, he snuggles, he kisses, he smells wonderful, and he loves sleeping between us under the covers with his head on the pillow.

But he ain't exactly smart.

Of course, I'm sure it doesn't build your confidence much to have a fat brother who gets everything before you do and takes your cookies and toys away from you constantly. We do our best to treat the boys with an even hand, and make sure Rascal doesn't take more than half of everything (including our attention).

But, you know, dogs will be dogs, and they behave how God made them behave.

Right?

I'm sure if we bothered to watch Cesar Millan, he'd teach us that this is the natural order of things and that Rascal has just established himself in the pecking order, which makes both dogs feel more comfortable and safe and know their roles in the pack. It's also possible that Ringo might be a different dog if he had a different brother (or perhaps different parents).

Which brings us to nurture: our parenting style. It's quite possible I *made* Ringo this way through bad parenting. Early on, when the dogs used to climb up on the Daddys' bed and destroy our pillows, I would go apeshit on them. I would yell and be hugely animated and put on a big show, yelling, "This is *Daddy's* pillow! Not Ringo's pillow! Not Rascal's pillow! *Daddy's* pillow!" Both dogs would quickly scurry into their house and look up at me guiltily. I thought they'd learn that Daddy doesn't like it when you destroy his pillow. Unfortunately, I think they learned something different than I intended.

I may have simply taught them that people are unpredictable and go into huge, loud, crazy temper tantrums for no good reason. Or at least that this Daddy does. Actually, the *other Daddy* begged me to calm down and not scare them. I wouldn't listen, though. I thought I was teaching them. Who knew?! Shit.

I'll have to remember not to make the same mistake with our future (human) children. In fact, I've promised my boyfriend that I've learned my lesson and will stick to the quiet, patient route from now on.

Sorry, doggies! I was a new parent. I didn't know any better. *Other Daddy* was right.

So, for whatever the reason, or some perfect storm of nature *and* nurture, here we are with one wonderful dog and one special dog. One Rascal and one Ringo.

But perhaps Ringo is here to teach us a spiritual lesson about accepting people as they are, not just the people we *like*. And this is where we try to apply our Rascal/Ringo dichotomy to people we meet out in the world. For us, when it comes down to it, everyone is either a Rascal or a Ringo. You just have to accept them and appreciate them for who they are.

When the shopkeeper tells you that he can't let you use the bathroom because it's "for employees only" and you do it anyway and he snaps at you and threatens to call the police, it's not that he's a rude little man; he was born that way and/or brought up that way. He's just *a Ringo*. Have compassion for him and love him. He probably snaps at everyone, and when he gets home he probably shakes and barks at the noises outside his window. Maybe he had a brother who stole all of his toys and food. He's probably a sweetie underneath, and if you only took the time to get to know him, you'd understand and want to let him sleep under the covers with you.

When the skinny, stupid airline representative tells you there are only middle seats left and she can't seat you and your boyfriend together, but says, "They might be able to reseat you at the gate" (yeah, right!), cut her some slack. She's just *a Ringo-Dingo*. Maybe she had an inexperienced young mother who yelled too much about destroying pillows and made her feel anxious and scared and rigid. Give her a Milk-Bone and scratch her belly. Maybe she'll feel more secure and end up being more compassionate.

By the same token, when the waiter is tall and friendly and handsome and says he loved *Avenue Q*, he's obviously *a Rascal*. Give him a big tip.

Despite their two very different personalities, we love both our Rascal and our Ringo unconditionally. They are who they are, whatever made them this way. Rascal may be more easy to love, but Ringo is just as lovable in his own special way. We just have to recognize the dogs for who they are and look for the best in both of them.

Remember the old adage, *beware of people who divide the world into chickens and foxes, for, to them, you are surely a chicken*? (No, most people don't know that saying, either. But trust me, I didn't make it up. Just like the thing about puppies in a litter having different fathers; it's real. I heard it somewhere.)

Anyway, all this may lead you to believe that my boyfriend and I both think of ourselves as Rascals. But it's not true.

I'd love to reveal which of us is which, but that's probably a bit too personal, don't you think?

Squatting with Stella by Starlight

Allie Larkin

I know I heard the words "fully trained" when the woman from the boarding kennel called a few days before Thanksgiving, asking us to adopt Luna. I am a gold medal champion when it comes to hearing only what I want to hear, but I do remember those words. And when I think back to that phone call, I am pretty sure the words "not even close to" didn't precede "fully trained," or "to drive you batshit crazy" didn't follow. In my mind, fully trained was supposed to mean that Luna answered to her name, sat when she was told to, peed outside like a good little dog, and possibly knew how to lie down on command. At least that's what fully trained meant in my mind. That's what I told my husband, Jeremy, while he was trying to shower. "We're getting another dog!" I shouted to him behind the shower curtain. "Don't worry! She's fully trained!" I said with complete confidence, when he poked his head out from behind the curtain, slightly panicked. "She even gets along fine with cats."

We already had one German shepherd. Argo came to us *fully trained* at five months, and was as sweet and perfect as could be.

For some reason, raising Argo from a perfect puppy to a perfect dog, in my mind, made me a German shepherd expert. I am, at least, a bronze medalist in thinking I know more about things than I actually do.

According to the lady at the kennel, Luna was not only fully trained, but she was small for a German shepherd. At thirteen months, she was pretty close to full grown, and in comparison to 105-pound Argo, she was tiny. If a 105-pound dog was easy, how much trouble could a 65-pound dog be, really? And, Luna was free. Her current owner worked too much and had to board Luna frequently at the same kennel where we left Argo when we went on vacation. She just wanted Luna to go to a good home. We wouldn't have to pay an adoption fee, or go through the home visits, fence construction, background checks, and promises of giving up our firstborn to get her, like we would if we went through an official rescue organization. If I had any doubts at all, they were completely quieted when the woman from the kennel said the magic words that would stroke any dog owner's ego to the point of compliance: "I told Luna's owner that if I had to give up one of my dogs, you guys are the people I would call."

We were the chosen ones. The fully trained little dog needed us.

Jeremy had a huge work project due right after Thanksgiving, so I took Argo out to the kennel to meet his new friend by myself. Luna was about half the size of Argo. She had beautiful traditional German shepherd markings, long skinny legs, a delicate nose, and ears that were too big for the rest of her, like a coyote. She cowered behind her owner when I tried to pet her, but when I sat on the floor, she marched over to me and licked my chin, like she realized right then and there that I was going to be the wonderful lady who would change her life.

We'd been looking for a second dog for months. When we finally thought we'd found the perfect dog for our family, a pretty little spaniel mix, and introduced her and Argo, she snarled and barked at him, leaving us all feeling a little rejected and insulted. Even though Argo had no interest in Luna, and was more interested in leaning against my legs and being clingy, Luna was fascinated by him. Her eyes filled with awe, her tail wagged. She trotted around him like she was dancing. It was beautiful, and it made me fall in love with her instantly. Anyone who loved my dog that much had to be a good egg.

Her owner arranged to drop her off at our house the next day, and I was so excited. I envisioned a bit of an adjustment, of course, but we'd been through that with Argo. When we first brought him home, he paced around the house for about twenty minutes to get his bearings. A few days later, he chewed a shoe, but when we scolded him in a slightly angry voice, he cowered in the corner and looked completely devastated. Otherwise, Argo fit seamlessly into our lives, making us laugh, giving us unconditional love and tons of sloppy dog kisses. And in my dog inexperience, I honestly thought that was the norm. That is what I expected from Luna. But as soon as Luna's owner left and I shut the door behind her, Luna morphed into a whirling mass of destruction, tipping over plants, chasing our poor old three-legged cat across the living room, knocking books off the bookshelves, chewing everything she could get her mouth around (including my arm), and herding Argo like a poor lost lamb until the only place he could stand without feeling her wrath was perched on the arm of the couch, like an elephant balanced on a ball at the circus. He looked as bewildered as I felt. Luna was like a turbocharged wild animal. I'd never seen anything like it.

"Luna!" I yelled. "Sit!"

"Rauooo!" she howled at me, before bounding off to chew on the leg of the coffee table.

"Luna! No!" I yelled.

She didn't even look at me.

"Luna!!!!"

Not even a glance my way.

Over the next few days, I learned some things about Luna. She did not know that her name was Luna. She did not have an understanding of any sort of "no" command. She would sometimes sit when told, but her success rate was so low it was quite possibly coincidence, not obedience. And while Argo hung on my every word, cocking his head from one side to the other while I talked, hoping the next thing I said would pertain to him, Luna didn't seem to understand that words could mean anything to her at all. She never made eye contact. She barely reacted to me.

And then there was the peeing. No matter how many trips around the block we took in freezing, Rochester winter weather, Luna would not pee. I spent hours walking her, teeth chattering, scared I'd slip on ice and crack my head open whenever she yanked at her leash to take off after a squirrel, or attempt to protect me from a fearsome three-year-old making snow angels. No matter how long it had been since she last relieved herself, Luna would not pee while she was on a leash. I started to worry that she might explode.

Luna would only pee in the backyard, off leash, after pacing around in circles for at least twenty minutes trying to find the exact right spot. The second she was done peeing, she'd take off, racing through the neighbors' yards, or down the street, or across the field behind our house, leaving me to chase her, yelling, at all hours of the night.

She'd pee perfectly in the backyard and come back in immediately like a little saint just often enough to fool me into thinking she'd gotten the routine down; of course, the next time I wouldn't bother to bundle up for the quick trip outside—and she'd choose to take off. I'd have to chase after her wearing slippers that would fly off my feet as I ran, and my ratty old pajama pants with a big hole down the side of one leg, letting the single-digit temperatures creep in and giving my neighbors a full display of my pathetic ineptitude.

By day, Luna needed to be watched constantly, so my days, which had previously been filled with work and cleaning, leisurely cups of tea, and occasional phone chats with friends, were suddenly completely consumed by the sole purpose of keeping Luna from chewing things and torturing our other pets.

At night, Luna would flail around her wire crate at the end of our bed. We knew sleeping in the same room was an important part of the bonding process, but Luna was the only one getting any rest. Even Argo couldn't sleep through her scratching and snoring. We were all sleep-deprived, except for Luna, who woke up every morning well rested and ready to take on another day of pulling stuffing out of a couch cushion, or chewing the corner of the living room rug like it was a good piece of jerky.

Jeremy's work project made him something of a stranger for the first month we had Luna. When he got home at night, he was greeted by me in tears, Argo nervously clutching his favorite toy in his mouth and growling under his breath, the cat puking in the corner, and our newest family member barking madly, lunging viciously at Jeremy, desperately trying to protect us all from him.

The day after Thanksgiving, after all the dishes were washed and the pots and pans put away, I made a mess of the kitchen all over again to roast an extra turkey I'd bought on holiday sale with plans of leftovers for easy meals and tasty dog treats.

While I cooked, Argo perched on the arm of the couch, the cat hid behind the toilet in the bathroom, and Luna pranced around, talking back at me with cries of "Rauooo!" anytime I told her to stop her current display of destruction. When the turkey finally finished cooking, I pulled it out of the oven and, distracted and sleep-deprived, tried to transfer it to a carving board, accidentally dousing my hand in boiling turkey fat in the process.

I put Luna in her crate and grabbed my purse so I could drive myself to the emergency room, ignoring her shrieks of protest and the clanging metal as she smashed her body up against the walls of the crate while I searched for my keys.

The emergency room, at eight p.m. on the day after Thanksgiving, seemed blissfully quiet and calm in comparison to being at home with Luna. My burn wasn't bad, and I was low-priority. An orderly put me in an out-of-the-way, curtained-off section, handed me a TV remote, and said, apologetically, "It's going to be a while."

"Not a problem," I said, earnestly. My hand hurt, but not so badly that I couldn't appreciate having my own little haven where reruns of *Family Ties* were playing on the television and no one was chewing on anything—at least not that I could see or was responsible for.

Two hours and a tetanus shot later, I was in my car and on my way home. My arm and hand throbbing, sorry to be returning to the zoo our house had become, I thought about taking a wrong turn, getting on the highway, and running away from home. It took every ounce of willpower I had to drive in the right direction, and when I pulled my car into the garage, I felt like my legs wouldn't work. I could not make myself go into the house. I sat in the car for almost an hour, listening to oldies on the radio and checking my e-mail on my cell phone, until it got too cold, and I started to worry I was draining the car battery. I felt like an idiot. I thought it was going to be easy to bring Luna into our lives. I thought it was going to be happy. I thought it would be good for Argo to have a friend, but he was miserable.

And then, of course, as soon as I walked in the door, I had to take Luna out to pee, and ended up chasing her through my neighbor's yard, trying to catch her with my unburned hand. She didn't even pee.

"We can't keep her," I whispered, sobbing later that night, when Jeremy came home and climbed into bed. "I can't do this anymore."

We agreed that I would call the kennel in the morning and tell them I couldn't keep her. As much as it was hard to live with her, I knew giving her back would leave a hole in my heart. I'd always have guilt, there'd always be an empty space. I'd always wonder what had happened to her. When we agreed to take her, I'd been assured that the kennel would try to find another home for her if it didn't work out. But how long would they try? When would they have to give up? I'd always fear the worst. But I didn't know what else to do. I didn't want to be a martyr for the next twelve years—at the expense of my sanity and the well-being of my home and family. She wouldn't look at me, she wouldn't listen to me, and I couldn't see how things could get better. In my mind, there was no amount of training that could ever take her from that crazy to anything even resembling a normal dog. And, because she was so aggressive on a leash, the idea of taking her to an obedience class seemed like an even more overwhelming nightmare. I couldn't stop thinking about it, and I couldn't sleep. So when Luna started whining at three a.m., I heard her right away, and took her outside to pee.

We walked around the yard, Luna's leash clutched in my nearly frozen hand, until I got so cold I couldn't stand it anymore. "Why can't you pee like a normal dog?" I cried. My teeth were chattering, and I couldn't feel my toes anymore. I crouched down and balled up, trying to conserve the little bit of heat I still had left in my body.

Luna trotted over and squatted next to me. I heard the trickle of pee hitting the frozen ground, and started giggling. It was weird, squatting next to a peeing dog. I realized that she thought I was peeing, too. When she finished, she licked my face. I cheered, "You did it! You are such a good dog!" Luna jumped around me, wagging her tail. I ran for the house. She followed me in without hesitation.

All she needed was to know that someone was there for her. I realized that I wasn't being a martyr in keeping her. I couldn't let her go. I needed her, too. I needed to be a better person, so she could be a better dog. I'd been so focused on everything she'd been doing wrong and everything she was supposed to be and wasn't, that I hadn't given her a chance to succeed. I expected her to take forever to pee and then run away, and she fulfilled that. But the second I supported her, even if it was accidental, she didn't want to run away. She wanted to be with me, and she wanted my praise. We just hadn't learned how to communicate with each other yet.

The next day, instead of arranging to give Luna back, I went to the library and checked out every book on dog behavior that I could find. I brought them home and read them while Luna snoozed on the couch next to me.

First, I realized, Luna needed a new name. She didn't have any positive associations with the word "Luna." I e-mailed Jeremy a list of names. "Does this mean you want to keep her?" he asked.

"I just want to try something," I told him.

We renamed her Stella, and I started walking around the house with treats in my pocket like all the books recommended. Every twenty minutes or so, I'd call "Stella!" and hand her a treat, even if she'd been standing right by me all along. It didn't take her long to understand that the word "Stella" meant good things. She was starting to realize that sometimes words related to her.

From my reading, I learned that Stella might benefit from having a job. So, every morning, no matter how cold or icy, I'd load up a doggie backpack with cans of beans and a small baggie of treats, strap it to Stella, and walk her around the block, trying my damnedest to be calm and assertive and be her best friend like the books told me. I circled the block in my winter boots and Yaktrax and tried not to think fearful thoughts of slipping on ice and cracking my skull open. If I didn't put my insecurities aside, she would take over, and I'd end up getting dragged down the street on my butt while she chased after a little old man shoveling snow. I needed to give her opportunities to succeed. She needed me to be a strong leader, and it forced me to be one.

When we got home, I'd load the beans back in the cupboard and give her the treats out of the baggie, praising her for her fine work. I don't know if it was the sense of purpose transporting beans around the block gave her, the payola she got at the end, or the simple fact that the backpack full of beans exhausted her more than just a regular walk, but when we got home, she was calmer, and ready to take a nap. She'd press her nose against my leg and snore while I sat on the couch with her and typed. I didn't care if it was crazy to walk around the block with a dog carrying beans like a pack mule. It was working.

Argo started to warm up to her, too. The toys he'd hide from her turned into his tools to entice her to play with him. He'd bring his favorite ball out in plain sight, dropping it on the hardwood floor so it would bounce over to Stella. She'd pick it up, run around with it, tail wagging, and drop it so it would bounce back to Argo. They would play like that for hours, stopping for impromptu naps and water breaks. It was noisy and raucous—the cat kept her distance, and I moved all things breakable out of the living room—but the sound of the bouncing ball and dog nails skittering on the floor was so much better than Argo's frustrated whimper and Stella's teeth scraping away at the leg of our coffee table. It was also better than the sound of Argo sighing around the ball in his mouth when he wanted to play and I needed to work. Stella still looked at Argo with those sweet brown eyes full of puppy love. When I told her to do something and she talked back at me with her big bellowing "Rauooo!" or yanked a houseplant out of its pot and dragged it across the living room floor, or pulled dirty tissues out of the wastepaper basket and left little bits of them strewn across every room in our house, I'd think, "At least she has good taste in dogs." I'd remind myself that Argo was a happier dog because of Stella. And gradually, I started to realize that I was a happier person because of Stella. She challenged me. She made me work for her obedience and I made her work for her praise. We balanced each other.

In the spring, as soon as the ground had thawed enough, we had our yard fenced in, so Stella could run around to her heart's content, but I spent that first winter with her, squatting in the backyard to give her moral support, for all the neighbors to see, in negative temperatures, snowstorms and starlight.

Peekapoo, Where Are You?

Annabelle Gurwitch

The late 1970s saw my family living in Wilmington, Delaware, where the powerful reach of the Dupont family and the company of the same name cast such a lengthy shadow that those who lived in its shade trudged through their existence in a sort of half-light.

At least that's how it seemed to me at age twelve.

But then I learned that we were moving south, and not just south, but to Miami Beach. I had no idea in how many ways this move would change our lives. We packed up our solidly middle-class redbrick walk-up apartment and landed in a brightly painted concrete and glass building (with an elevator!), where we were to stay for several weeks until we could enter the home my dad had found for us. It was as though we'd been trapped in a black-and-white film and suddenly we woke up in Technicolor. From the moment we landed, Miami was an assault on the eyes and senses.

I can't remember every detail of my wedding day, but I can that first day in Miami, from my heart beating excitedly on the ride up to the penthouse apartment to the thrilling moment we crossed the threshold into a living facsimile of Barbie's Malibu Dream House.

The joint was sparsely furnished, everything modern, clean, and mostly white. A white plastic chair in the shape of a hand was in one corner, strands of silver love beads separated the kitchen and dining area, and a metal spiral staircase led to the loft bedrooms upstairs. Floor-to-ceiling glass doors opened onto a gravel rooftop balcony that looked out onto a park below. The park was landscaped with majestic royal palms, the stately wide palm trees that I had only seen in episodes of *The Beverly Hillbillies*.

This could mean only one thing: We were rich!

It couldn't have been further from our apartment in Delaware, which backed up to a large cement drainage pipe in whose runoff— water whose provenance was unknown—I regularly played, which I'm fairly certain is not at all responsible for the fact that I am a good three to four inches shorter than all of my blood relations, but is still, nonetheless, troubling. The uniting design feature of the rental unit was Day-Glo yellow and orange deep-pile shag carpeting that covered every inch of floor space, even in the bathrooms.

The day we arrived I lay down on that neon acrylic expanse next to the sliding glass doors and let the sun warm my sallow skin.

That's when I noticed the carpet was damp.

Now, if it had been only a day earlier, I might have speculated that this was due to an unfortunate instance of impatience on the part of our pooch Petey.

Petey was our Peekapoo, a breed I had never heard of when we acquired him and have heard little of since. The Peekapoo is sort of an also-ran hybrid, like a car I would later own, the Chevy Monza. With the wheelbase of a Vega and the engine of a Corvair,

Chevrolet made that clunker for only five years before they concluded, "Well, that didn't work," and chucked it.

The Pekinese-poodle hybrid has been around for about half a century now, but a Peekapoo has still never sold a burrito or a beer, never starred in a movie, never been memorialized into a Monopoly token, and never been a member of a royal family, like the flirtier and more popular Pomeranian, several of which accompanied Queen Victoria everywhere she went.

One of the most prominent features of the Peekapoo is what has been termed its hilarious attachment to its owners. The way this manifested itself in our Peekapoo was that our dog liked to be with us so much he often urinated on the floor rather than go outside and be separated.

Our Petey was basically a barking ball of stringy hair that collected everything in his path. Leaves, twigs, crumbs, even poop were regularly found clinging to his scrawny little body. His smashed Pekinese nose was often runny. He was basically a mess, but that didn't dampen his enthusiasm for us.

Pee ka poo.

Maybe not such a good name for a breed.

That shag carpet turned out to share the collective quality of our dog, but Petey never got to dig into its mysterious depths because he wasn't with us. He'd be taking a later flight and meeting us in Florida soon. At least, that's what my sister and I were told.

He was taking a later flight.

He'd be rejoining our family.

When?

Soon.

The excuse that Petey would be jetting in on a later flight didn't seem so far-fetched. We had a lot of stuff. Sure, I mean, why not, anything was possible, after all: We'd resided in gray-flanneled Delaware and now we were in acid-washed Miami Beach? The world was magical, we'd landed in paradise, and a dog could fly unaccompanied on an airplane. Sounded possible. To a twelve-year-old.

Then, a letter arrived addressed to my sister and myself.

Dear Anne and Lisa,

I am fine, I miss you, but I will not be joining you in Florida. I am living with your dad's secretary, Caroline. I have had such a good time staying here that I don't want to leave. I have become Italian and I love spaghetti. We have it a lot!

Love,
Petey

It was signed with a paw print.

I'm not proud of admitting this, but I loved being mad at parents. Like many children, I carried the vague sense that a great injustice had been done by just being born into my family, and this letter gave my anger focus. Which was worse? The idea that my dog had chosen another family over ours because they ate spaghetti on a regular basis, or that my parents would think up this kind of ruse?

I cried and cried, but a parental decision had been made. In a short time, we no longer looked twice at the palm trees that dotted the beach, and my sister and I—in our matching Nik Nik polyester shirts—soon learned to craft tanning reflectors out of tinfoil, learned how to blow-dry our hair like Farrah, and learned that

Soylent Green was made of people, so life went on. But over the years, I loved telling the story of how my parents had sucked, and I had proof, the tangible evidence of one of the many wrongs that had been inflicted upon me.

Cut to thirty years later, just a few months after our cat Esme took to living in the shrubbery in front of the home I share with my husband and son. Esme was a foundling who spent most of her time cowering in the deepest recesses of our closets, so that she earned the nickname "Fraidy Cat." When our psychotic cat had first exiled herself to the bushes, I was so desperate that I consulted a pet psychic. Pet Psychic Lady only charged $125 to inform me that the cat was being bombarded by negative thoughts from an old boyfriend of mine. Oh, and on top of that we needed to start calling the cat by her given name.

"Would you come if you were called Fraidy?" she admonished me.

"No," I answered, "but I also don't come running when I hear a can being opened."

Pet Psychic Lady didn't have a sense of humor, but she didn't need one; after all, she had people like me paying good money for her advice.

I actually held out hope that this would work right up until the night my husband and I were watching television together and we heard a small yelp. Jeff went outside and saw a coyote trotting away with Esme/Fraidy Cat limp in his mouth.

The next day our five-year-old son, Ezra, inquired where Fraidy Cat had gone. Before I could think, I heard myself saying that sometimes when an animal is sick, it crawls off to die alone and that's exactly what happened with Esme. That was the answer that I stuck with for the first day.

The next morning more questions came. "Where did she go?"

"She went to the side of a canyon near our home."

But wait, there's more!

"I want to see where she went to die."

"Of course, sweetheart, we'll visit the spot at dusk. It has a beautiful view, and is very peaceful."

As my son and I stood on the hillside, looking out at the national park that borders our neighborhood, where in truth, Esme's remains probably do reside, it hit me: There was not a royal palm in sight, just scrub bush and sage. No elaborate scheme had been hatched, but sure enough, I had "Peteyed" my own child.

At that moment, I realized I'd have to forgive my parents. Sure, maybe it was ill conceived and, in truth, rather poorly executed. I mean, why was the letter signed with a *paw print*; if Petey had actually composed the rest of the note himself, he could have signed his name as well. And sure, maybe that incident explained why, as an adult, I had shunned canine companionship and turned to feline felicity. My parents were trying to soften the blow of the loss of a pet, and now I wanted to shield my offspring from a loss as well. I sighed and breathed in the cool evening air. Who knows, I thought, there might be a dog in this family's future yet.

Pimping Out Delilah

Sarah Pekkanen

It was obvious: Delilah needed a boyfriend.

I was in the fifth grade when our pug began sexually assaulting the shinbones of everyone who dared to enter our house.

So with the determination of an old-school religious couple setting up an arranged marriage, my parents began soliciting a gigolo for our pudgy, cantankerous, two-year-old dog.

The first family to respond to our call offered up Cagney, a genial, doddering fellow who had the befuddled air of someone who was perpetually searching for his eyeglasses. In hindsight, I think Cagney's family might've been using us as a pet-sitting service, because Cagney was not what one might call "goal-oriented." By the time he arrived at our house—accompanied by his plush bed and teddy bear—Delilah was delirious with excitement. She waited on the couch, her Dibs-shaped body quivering with lust, for Cagney to amble arthritically by. Exhibiting the timing and fearlessness of a movie stunt double, Delilah would then leap onto Cagney's back, her hips churning like Britney Spears's.

But Cagney was unimpressed by Delilah's gymnastic prowess

and gyrations, and flopped down for a siesta while she went in search of an unsuspecting leg. He pretty much stayed asleep until his family, tanned and rested and smelling vaguely of piña coladas, came to pick him up a week later.

The next time Delilah went into heat, my parents again cast a wide net for a pug—any pug—to mate with her and provide us kids with the free sex-education lessons that they, being borderline hippies, felt were our right.

An elderly woman volunteered her dog, imaginatively named Puggy, and although we were wary, he was the only stud on the horizon. So my mother piled my two brothers and me into our ancient station wagon and we drove fifty miles to pick up Delilah's suitor, fighting the entire way about who had crossed the imaginary lines separating our seats.

After we entered the woman's house, which boasted a decorating scheme of dozens and dozens of lace doilies, the woman bypassed pleasantries and issued one nonnegotiable order: Puggy was to have a pack of gum each day.

"Gum?" asked my bewildered mother.

"Juicy Fruit," Puggy's owner specified, filling our hands with bright yellow packages. "He just loves it."

She paused in doling out the goods to give us the stink eye, and one of my brothers surreptitiously put back the doily he was trying to steal. "Don't you kids go and chew it yourselves."

"No, ma'am," we blurted, our faces as angelic as those on the Precious Moments collectible dolls the old lady had showcased atop the doilies.

We barely made it to the car before we fell upon the bounty like starving jackals, shoving entire packs into our mouths. By the time we pulled into our driveway, we resembled hyperactive chipmunks. Our mouths were so full that none of us could talk without lisping profoundly.

Deprived of his beloved Juicy Fruit, the obese Puggy slumped around, sighing morosely. Delilah would've turned up her nose at him if it hadn't already been permanently flattened into that position against her face, and refused to go near him. Once the gum was gone and we realized that was the only trick in his repertoire, we kids lost interest in Puggy, too, and he spent the rest of the visit perched on our couch like another overstuffed throw pillow, watching sporting events with my father.

Luckily, Rocky was waiting in the wings, like the perfect suitor who swoops in during the final scenes of a rom-com movie. The couple that owned Rocky worked long hours and knew he wasn't getting the attention he deserved. They wanted to sell him for $250. But my family couldn't afford him, and we left their house dejectedly, having already fallen in love with his sweet manner and random, explosive snorts. A few hours later, the couple phoned, saying they'd take $50 because they loved the idea of Rocky going to a bustling, happy home with the side benefit of unlimited sex.

Rocky—swiftly renamed Sampson—snored louder than any man I've ever met and awoke with the same furtive look as my father when caught napping: *I was just resting my eyes!* He also routinely passed gas that would halt conversation as everyone fled the room, shirt collars pulled up over noses and mouths. But he approached Delilah with the grim determination of a man hired to do a job and do it well. Within a day, we suspected Delilah was knocked up.

Sampson, however, wasn't finished. Across the street lived Delilah's twin, Spunky. Apparently Hugh Hefner isn't the only one who appreciates the allure of sisters, because soon Sampson was slinking under her fence, perhaps drawn by the tantalizing promise inherent in Spunky's name.

Within a few months, both sisters produced litters of pugs, and Sampson seemed to have a special strut in his step. Being reasonable people, our neighbors quickly found good homes for all of their pug puppies. My parents, however, were already beaten down by us three kids. We cajoled and wheedled until they promised we could keep one of the three puppies.

"But just one," they repeated, with all the confidence of people who were used to having their pronouncements ignored.

Since Delilah liked my older brother, Robert, the best, and Sampson and I had bonded, it was decided that Ben, the baby of the family, would get to pick which puppy we kept.

From early on, his choice was clear: While all three puppies were insanely adorable (I defy you to find anything cuter than a pug puppy), one was downright spectacular. Alfonzo, as Ben named him in a rebellion against our biblical theme, was pure white, not the dirty-snow color of the other pugs. His eyes were large and as luminous as an Italian lover's, and his chest was broad and curved.

Alfonzo's tail also curled over on itself twice. "The prized double-kink!" my father often proclaimed, displaying an inexplicable knowledge of show-dog terminology.

My father seemed to take a particular pride in Alfonzo. He had children who humiliated him at every turn—once we pulled down his pants in the middle of the grocery store; another time, he was summoned to my elementary school because my teacher wanted to show him exactly how messy my desk was—but he would have this one shining triumph in life: He would have the most beautiful pug on the block.

And beautiful he was. Had it been possible for him to compete, Alfonzo would be awarded the Junior Miss tiara. More than that, he'd taken an immediate liking to Ben. He followed Ben around faithfully, sat by his feet while Ben ate dinner, and would only sleep on Ben's bed. My parents watched the two of them frolicking in the yard together in the manner of a laundry detergent commercial, and knew the choice was a given.

Then Ben spoke up. "I'm keeping McDuff," he declared.

My parents wheeled around to face one another, then with the simultaneous precision of soldiers, spun out to stare at Ben. "McDuff?" they repeated.

McDuff was the runt of the litter. He had no double kink in his tail; it just sort of flopped there, like a giant piece of overcooked rigatoni. He was small and scrawny, and his eyes bulged out disconcertingly. His head was oddly shaped, too, with a few knobby bumps and one flat spot just above the eyes. He resembled E.T. without the lit-up finger.

"Don't you want to keep Alfonzo?" my parents wheedled.

Ben shook his head, and stood his ground in his Toughskins jeans. "McDuff."

"But Alfonzo loves you," my mother said.

"The double-kink tail!" my father moaned.

Ben smiled. "Nope."

By now Robert and I understood what was unfolding.

"McDuff's a great dog," Robert said.

"Good choice," I added.

"Christ!" my father bellowed, his universal signal for conceding an argument. He stormed off to watch television, and Robert and I high-fived Ben. We all knew we were keeping McDuff *and* Alfonzo.

As it turned out, McDuff had the best personality of all of our dogs. Delilah, never a peach, grew more curmudgeonly and delusional as she aged, often picking vicious fights with bedding or large rocks. Alfonzo had beauty-queen looks but, true to stereotype, no brains (once, he tore across the lawn and smashed facefirst into the hubcap of our car, which was parked in the driveway). And Sampson, while noble, could be hot-tempered and obstinate, as well as an unabashed adulterer.

But McDuff was a prince. He was the last one to bed at night, faithfully yawning alongside whoever stayed up late, and the first one to rise in the morning, joining my mother on the couch at dawn while she knocked back the copious amounts of caffeine she needed to steel herself for the day ahead. While the other pugs slept curled up in the curves behind our bent knees, like snorting, farting Hot Pockets, McDuff stayed alert in case someone in the house had insomnia and needed company. If anyone wandered into the kitchen for a midnight snack, they'd hear the scrabble of nails on the linoleum floor and look down to see McDuff's gentle bug eyes blinking up at them.

McDuff was a lover, not a fighter (unlike Delilah, who was both, and continued molesting shins even after my parents deemed us sufficiently educated and had her spayed). Whenever the other pugs got into a scrap, which happened like clockwork at every mealtime when bowls of kibble were set down, McDuff would hurl his bony body into the middle of the fracas. His good intentions never lasted, however, for as soon as he was nipped, he'd morph from Gandhi into Cujo, joining in the snapping and yowling while my parents shouted ineffective threats and pulled the pugs apart.

Invariably, moments after their squabble was halted, all four pugs would converge again on the same bowl, while my mother gestured to three untouched, identical bowls like a manic Home Shopping Network showgirl. My parents were the only ones who ever got hurt during the pug fights, since the dogs had thick fur and tiny mouths and never inflicted damage on each other.

"Jesus!" my father would shout at the pugs, nursing a freshly bitten thumb. "There are four bowls of food. *Four!* That's one each!"

The pugs would endure these mathematical lectures by staring dourly at my father, and occasionally passing gas.

Since my dad is a writer who works at home, the soundtrack to many of his business calls were snarls and yips. Once, while breaking apart a squabble with one hand and clutching the phone to his ear with the other, he could hear the editor on the other end of the line muffling hysterical laughter. Dad's patience was wearing thin, so my parents came up with the brilliant idea of halting the spats by leaving food out *all the time*, so the dogs could just snack whenever they pleased (somewhere, Cesar Millan is reading this and weeping). The idea worked for about ten minutes. Then, a pug wandered over to sniff at a bowl, another pug got up to see what was so interesting, and a fresh battle commenced.

Taking our pugs for a walk was no less dramatic than feeding them. For some reason, my parents refused to use leashes, presumably because their borderline hippie personalities meant they couldn't stand to see anything restrained. Since none of the pugs was particularly smart—more than once, when my father stopped to talk to a neighbor, a pug would amble over, mistake the neighbor's leg for a tree, and pee on it—our walks were a spectacle. First our front door would fly open, then the pugs would waddle out, followed by one or both of my parents, who would wave their arms and screech in an attempt to herd the pugs into the same general direction.

But the real excitement came when a car rounded the corner near our house.

"Grab a pug!" my parents would scream at bewildered passersby.

My father would then heroically attempt to block the car's progress with his body, dancing across the width of the street with his arms outstretched, while my mother frantically raced around, tucking pugs under her armpits in the same way that I've seen classy French women carry around baguettes.

Despite the close calls with cars, our pugs all lived long, happy lives. One by one, though, they succumbed to old age, until only McDuff was left. He remained faithful and steadfast to the very end, hobbling around on legs bowed from arthritis and waiting patiently to be lifted up on the couch alongside my mother as she sipped her morning coffee.

We buried him in our backyard, his little body nestled inside a pillowcase, next to the graves of his parents and brother.

Pictures of the pugs are still scattered around my parents' house, and even though it has been twenty years since McDuff died in my mother's arms while I was away at college, every time I open their door, I still reflexively look down, expecting to see their fat, wiggling bodies converging around my legs. But the house is quiet now; my parents dog-sit for their children's pets, but they've never gotten another pug.

Experts tell us the strongest portal to memory is our sense of smell, but for me, it's a certain sight that brings my childhood rushing back. Whenever I see someone walking a pug, I instinctively run toward them. I can't stop running my fingers over the soft wide forehead and staring into the gentle brown eyes. Instantly, I'm eleven years old again, feeling the steady warmth against me while I lie in bed, and listening to the gentle snorting lullaby that never failed to put me to sleep.

Pugs weren't just my childhood.

They were the best parts of it.

Wuzsha, Wuzsha, Wuzsha!

Eddie Sarfaty

As my father helped Donna coax Ginger into the Pooch Parlor with a Liv-A-Snap, I ran out of the garage dragging Cindy by the collar.

"Dad, Cindy needs her hair done, too."

"We'll give her a bath later."

"She needs a cut—she has split ends."

"I don't think Donna has time today."

"She might."

My father looked at me, and deciding it was worth the extra money to avoid listening to a twelve-year-old boy whine all day, turned to the bony blonde.

"Do you have time?"

Donna gave me a wink as she tightened her teddy bear barrette, exposing the gray roots of her sun-ravaged hair.

"Sure, not a problem."

"She needs her nails cut, too," I urged.

"We'll give her the works."

Cindy wasn't easily lured into the calamine pink van, and

Donna's assistant, a pudgy girl in a tube top, had to hoist the scruffy black mutt into the back. As she was closing the parlor's rear doors, adorned with a snooty poodle, I heard Donna whisper to the girl, "This one'll be a breeze—she hardly needs anything." She had the air of a kiddie-pageant official who's smilingly accepted an entrance fee from the deluded parents of a homely third-grader.

Despite Donna's remark, I was thrilled Cindy was getting the royal treatment instead of her usual cold-water shower with the garden hose and Prell shampoo. I wanted her to feel pretty, too—and not like the Baby Louise to Ginger's Baby June.

Every other month, Donna parked the pink monstrosity in the driveway of our assembly-line Long Island house as she bathed, cut, and blew Ginger dry. Between groomings, I was supposed to brush the golden retriever regularly to avoid knots and to minimize the tumbleweeds of shed fur that swirled around the house. Ginger was beautiful. Athletic, with a glossy, amber coat, she reminded me of the thoroughbred-legged boys who shone in gym class and the popular girls who were forever combing their Farrah Fawcett hair.

Although Ginger was as cuddly as a Muppet, I didn't feel a particularly strong attachment to her. My failure to force my Jew-fro into a satisfactory approximation of the '70s feathered style and my self-consciousness about my fat-boy boobs made it easier for me to identify with Cindy's kinky hair and goofy proportions. Knowing firsthand the sting of being shunned by the cool kids in junior high, I was determined Cindy should never feel slighted. After I finished attending to Ginger, I always brushed Cindy's raggedy pelt the same number of strokes—eventually irritating her skin and causing a bald patch on her rump.

Ginger had originally belonged to my aunt Syl and uncle Lenny, who'd paid more for the pedigreed dog than my parents paid for the used Dodge my father drove. Ginger had papers proving she was descended from champions—and so was supposedly better than Cindy, whom we'd rescued from a cinder-block shelter. I never questioned that Ginger was more important; it made sense to me. Syl and Lenny's brick house was bigger than our wooden one, their yard was landscaped, their furniture matched. My cousins Elliot and Tracy took swimming lessons at a ritzy country club, while I had to repeatedly fling my Frisbee into the neighbors' yard, hoping to get invited into their tin-can pool. Syl and Lenny had been to Sweden and Italy; my parents had been to Hershey, Pennsylvania. Plus, my grandmother—whom I adored—had chosen to live with their family. Why wouldn't she?

But as I learned, nobody gets through life unscathed, and good fortune can vanish at any moment. In five years, the better family in the brick house was no more. A sudden heart attack, a suicide, and an aggressive cancer robbed Elliot of his father, sister, and mother. Even now, over thirty years later, I can still hear Aunt Syl's wails, muffled against my father's shoulder, as she stood beside Lenny's newly planted plot and watched her eldest child being lowered into the autumn ground. And I'll never forget the misery in my grandmother's face on the September morning four years later when, in the same tiny cemetery, she buried Syl. I also clearly recall the day Granny and Elliot came to live with us, pulling up to the curb with the last load of their belongings—and with Ginger, who gleefully bounded across our lawn, seemingly oblivious to the enormous changes in all our lives.

It never occurred to me that the tragedies of those five years had any effect on bouncy, purebred, inbred Ginger. Dismissing her as insensitive was easy since I'd already cast her in the role of the pretty girl who only cared about being admired. When she started eating anything she could sniff on the shallow kitchen counter (even once, an entire seven-pound Hebrew National salami, plastic and string included)—and then quietly vomiting in a corner—it was easy to write her off as a narcissistic blonde with an eating disorder.

Cindy employed her sense of smell more intelligently, carefully assessing every scrap of food first instead of just gobbling up anything that wasn't nailed down. She was talented enough to find survivors in the rubble after an earthquake, if necessary. Ginger, I'm certain, would only be able to locate victims fortunate enough to be buried with a box of Snausages. Though there was no fence between our yard and Artie the cop's next door, Cindy knew exactly where our property ended and would automatically halt even if you kept walking. Ginger would stop only when her nose was bored or the continental shelf ended. Cindy would routinely receive a biscuit after performing a variety of neat tricks in quick succession. All Ginger had to do for a reward was sit—after being told five times to stop jumping on the company. The inequity reinforced what I was learning in school: Looks matter—a lot.

On one of my grandmother's first mornings with us, as I was showing her how I make chocolate milk with the last of my Cocoa Puffs, my mom, engrossed in the paper, was mindlessly scratching Cindy under the chin. Ginger, as usual demanding to be the center of attention, wedged herself between them, and Cindy, without dejection, trotted off, accepting her new standing like a faithful old housekeeper quietly performing her duties when the pretty new chambermaid catches the mistress's attention. Ginger reveled in the attention while my mom tousled her ears, kissed her on the snout, and whispered, "What is it, pretty girl? What is it? Yes, you've been through a lot. I know, I know."

Whenever she spoke to Ginger that way, I'd get furious at my mom's lack of sensitivity. Sure, Ginger had been through a lot, but what about Cindy? She'd been abandoned, possibly abused, and had languished in a filthy shelter for God knows how long. That Cindy was so accepting of her second-class status made me crazy.

I also hated the way Ginger shamelessly threw herself at my father, who, despite his macho-free demeanor, was the alpha dog in our family pack. His return from the office had always been the big event in Cindy's day, but with Ginger going mental, pawing him and whimpering in ecstasy the moment he walked through the door, Cindy resigned herself to her new place in the pecking order. She'd stand a few feet back, waiting patiently for Ginger's fit to subside and for my dad to give her a few seconds of attention before he kissed my mom and looked in the refrigerator.

Twenty minutes after the two dogs had been taken into the Pooch Parlor, Cindy emerged from her makeover. Although Donna charged my dad for the complete spa package, there wasn't much different about Cindy's appearance. But I fussed over her manicured nails and, assuring her how elegant she was, kissed her repeatedly. The poor thing seemed embarrassed by the attention—like a tomboy in a puffy bridesmaid's dress—and curled up under a tree to wait for Ginger to make her entrance.

Finally, half an hour later, Ginger, shiny and manageable, bolted out of the van, eager to show off her new do. The girl in the tube top fawned over her as she gave Ginger a final once-over with a metal comb. "You are such a beauty! You're gonna have gorgeous babies!"

"She's fixed," I yelled.

"What a shame, you could've made some nice money."

I hated the girl and her wrinkly belly. I knew she'd never say that about Cindy—nobody would. The morning my mom and her friend Jen Wolfberg took Cindy to get spayed, I begged them to let her have puppies and was told by Jen, "The last thing we need are more unwanted animals that need to be euthanized." I wanted to spay Jen.

We humans are often unaware of our own prejudices, and it would never occur to a lot of us that there might be anything wrong with treating a dog differently because of its looks. What does it matter anyway? It's just a dog. They're inferior to us; on the tree of life, they're on a lower branch; canine brains are less than one-fifth the size of ours.

True, but this size difference has more to do with our highly developed neocortex, which allows us to reason, and less to do with the limbic system (the evolutionarily earlier sections of the brain that dogs and people have in common), from which emotions arise.

And aren't our emotions what make it a joy—or at least a profound experience—to be human? The ability to do algebra or write poetry has its advantages, but no matter how elegant a quadratic equation or well-crafted a sonnet, neither penetrates my heart as deeply as a wet nose and a wagging tail. If I ever had to choose between surrendering my intelligence or my feelings, the decision would be easy: I'd rather be an idiot than a sociopath.

Dogs avoid the great human quandary of reconciling their emotions with their intellect. They know exactly what to do. Comforting without hesitation and confronting without second-guessing themselves, they manage to live in the moment without "Just for today" tucked into the corner of the bureau mirror. Aside from Wile E. Coyote, canids are guileless.

I realized all of this that evening, after the chubby girl helped Donna maneuver the Pooch Parlor out of our driveway, and my parents left to play cards at their friends'. It was the night I fell in love with Ginger.

Standing at the sink, slathering cream cheese on the chocolate chip cookies my mother had hidden in the vegetable crisper, I could hear my grandmother in her room off of the kitchen wake up from "just resting my eyes." When her TV didn't immediately come on, I poked my head in the door. Granny, her bad hearing allowing me to spy, was seated on her upholstered green rocker, staring into silence, the cemetery expression ruining her face. She gazed down at the table beside her, at a photo of Syl and Lenny at Tracy's sweet sixteen, and sighed. At the sound, Ginger, snoozing in the corner, looked up and raised her ears. "Some life, huh, Gingie?"

At the mention of her name, Ginger jumped to her feet and threw her front half into my grandmother's lap. Granny laughed and tried to dodge the berserk animal's flank-steak tongue as Ginger covered her with kisses. But the big dopey thing knew what the old woman needed and, with unfettered affection, pulled Granny out of her memories and into the cold-nosed present.

When the licking finally ceased, my grandmother burrowed her nose into the dog's thick mane. "Wuzsha, wuzsha, wuzsha! Wuzsha, wuzsha, wuzsha!" And Ginger, burning the remaining adrenaline off with her tail, barked approvingly, causing Granny to laugh and launch a kissing assault of her own.

I stepped back into the kitchen unnoticed and sat quietly at the table, replaying the scene in my mind to ensure it would never be lost to me.

A year later the big Snuffleupagus was gone. Ginger's hind legs suddenly gave out (a common glitch when humans try to breed "perfect" dogs), and my parents had to put her down while I was on a school choir trip. My grandmother was heartbroken. Elliot had gone off to college by then, and Ginger had been the only one left who'd gone through the devastating losses with her.

I was angry my parents didn't call me home to say good-bye, and I spent the next two days sitting in Ginger's favorite place on the sofa, where I could still smell her. After two or three vacuumings, however, her scent was expunged, and the only pieces of evidence proving she'd been there were a chewed-up plastic frankfurter with a broken squeak and the little haystacks of hair we came across when we cared enough to sweep behind the furniture.

Though I loved Cindy, and was happy to see her shake off her timidity and reclaim her rightful position, I initially equated her exuberance with that of an aging Broadway diva called in to save the show when the starlet who'd replaced her falls ill. But after witnessing the delight that she, too, brought to Granny's face, it dawned on me that perhaps Cindy, the smartest and most sensitive of creatures, had simply been stepping back to allow Ginger— and the rest of us—to have what we all needed.

It was another year before I first noticed Cindy's muzzle beginning to gray, and over the next several years—as I shot up and finally slimmed down—the thud of her paws on the linoleum gradually changed to a dainty clacking. After Ginger, the pink van stopped coming around, and bathing Cindy became an increasingly important experience for me—far preferable to trusting her to Donna, who had dollar signs in her eyes. I loved the aging mutt unreservedly, but with a tinge of melancholy that scored my heart, preparing it for the inevitable break to come.

After the poor thing had limped arthritically into old age, she began having seizures. Though she bounced back somewhat between episodes, the attacks increased in frequency and severity until, finally, we had to acknowledge "it was time."

We put her down the day before I left for college.

Before we took her to the vet's, my dad shot a roll of film of Cindy and me on our front stoop. The guilt I felt getting her to look into the camera for her final portrait was excruciating. The feeble twitching of her tail brought me to the brink of tears, and I was only able to keep from breaking down completely because I couldn't bear to have a photo of my own face with an expression of grief I'd never be able to forget. As I dug my nose into her fur and rocked my head back and forth—"Wuzsha, wuzsha, wuzsha!"—I took a deep breath, aware that, as with Ginger, I'd soon be unable to recall Cindy's comforting scent.

In the years since Ginger and Cindy, I've lost Granny and my dad. Occasionally, at a party, or perhaps on the subway or in an elevator, a stranger's White Shoulders perfume or Old Spice aftershave will trigger specific memories of them. But it's been over thirty years since I've caught a whiff of anything that conjures up that magnificent show dog or that clever mutt.

Too bad nobody makes a cologne called Old Dog.

My Dog,
the Dominatrix

Jenny Gardiner

When I think about it, it's a wonder our rescue dog didn't come into our lives wielding a leather whip, sporting black patent leather thigh-high boots and a spiked collar. While the accoutrements of her temperament did not accompany her, the dominatrix collar would come, eventually. Only to her chagrin, it would be at her expense.

Bridget—our dingo–mush dog mash-up—came to us ready-made with *issues*. So much so that early in our relationship, a friend gave us a book on how to live with a neurotic dog: Everyone in our circle of friends knew that Bridget required coping skills far beyond what's required for your average mutt.

An impulse acquisition just a little too soon after the loss of our first dog, Bridget made up for in cute what she lacked in social acceptability. From a litter of abandoned five-week-old pups left on the side of the road to die, Bridget's survival skills held her in good stead long enough to be rescued; her mesmerizing gemstone blue pie eyes gave her the edge in landing a group of suckers who didn't quite need a high-maintenance dog, but would never dream of giving her up once in their care. That would be us: the Gardiners, who never met a pet they wouldn't go to the ends of the earth for, against all logic.

Now some of you may know about my family because of my memoir about our demanding African gray parrot, Graycie, a surprise gift some twenty years ago (the gift that keeps on giving, we like to say). Between our three small children (a fourth, if you count Graycie, with the intelligence and manipulative skills of a clever toddler), a few doddering cats with failing kidneys, and a not-even-back-from-the-crematory dead dog, by the time Bridget came along, we were up to our eyeballs in creatures that needed our undivided attention.

Despite yearning for a break from dog maintenance, lingering in the back of my mind when confronted with the immediate prospect of taking home this adorable pooch was the mantra I'd heard so often in my life about how great adopted dogs are.

"Get a pound pup!" people would advise (unsolicited, mind you). "They make the best pets. They're so grateful for your love, and *much* more well behaved."

I'm fairly sure these are the same people who'd assured me that my oversized nine-plus-pound newborn would sleep through the night in a matter of days (versus the nine months it took). In any event, Bridget must not have gotten that memo.

Bridget is sharp, both in intellect and appearance. There are no soft, smooth, family-dog curves to her. She's seemingly made up purely of geometric angles, from her long narrow snout and her pointy ears—prone to shift position like satellite antennae when discerning noises—to her angular haunches, which jut up like shark fins when she's poised in permanent ready-to-pounce mode. The only curve to her is her bushy tail, which arches in a regal semicircle, the tip of which sometimes dusts the food on our dinner plates when she walks beneath the table at mealtime.

I've always thought Bridget had the intellect and guile to work in counterintelligence were she human; she's savvy, intuitive, sometimes too smart for her own good. Even at the ripe age of eleven, our girl is perpetually at the ready, void of the capacity to rest at will. Too much to do, too much to be wary of. Rarely does she sleep lying on her side; relaxation does not come easily to her.

Bridget came with three pronounced problems that needed correction: dominant aggression (who knew that snippy pups became bitey dogs? Labradors never do!); severe wanderlust (which meant containing a creature with the single-minded determination to escape theretofore only seen in Allied POWs); and incessant barking (the latter two no doubt being mere subsets of her dominatrix spirit).

The aggression surprised us—we'd brought home an extremely docile puppy. Hell, those first few days, we could've bitten *her* and she wouldn't have complained, sleeping peacefully in our laps as she did. But once we de-wormed her and got rid of a bad case of temperament-suppressing parasites, Bridget morphed from mild-mannered to *wild*-mannered, so dominant she even lifted her leg to pee. So dingo-dominant we took to regularly saying with a pronounced *put-another-shrimp-on-the-barbie* accent, "Dingo ayte mah baybay" when in her presence. She'd put any male dog to bitter shame, hands down. Our first task was to dominate the hell out of the dog by poking, prodding, picking, pulling, and otherwise letting her know we were her bosses. This worked, to the surprise of the vet who'd warned us to give her away because her aggression could be dangerous. But we could never have cast aside a pup our family had fallen in love with, and so we worked within her constraints. Sure, maybe she transferred her dominance of people to dogs, but *that* we could live with.

By then the kids had taken to calling her Lulu, a highly extrapolated bastardization of some Portuguese term of endearment our Brazilian neighbor used with her daughters. It sounded something like *pichulinha*, which the kids changed to Poochaleenia, which then became Smoochie Pooch, which then became Looch, which then became Loochie, which then became Lulu. For good measure we threw in the middle name of Louise, so that when it came time to chastise her for bad behavior (a frequent happening), we had just the right cadence: a commanding *"Bridget Louise Gardiner"* in a stern voice that seemed to elicit far more respect than merely hollering *"Lulu!"*

With the dominance at least in check, we had to address her unrequited wanderlust, so that Bridget didn't end up on the wrong end of a hunter's rifle in the plentiful woods surrounding our home (even *I* have mistaken her tan, rust, and black camouflage coat for a fleeing deer amid the autumn woods), or meet a premature end courtesy of a passing car. Used to her freedom since infancy, being contained in an acre-sized yard was practically solitary confinement for Bridget, whom we'd learned was part Blue Heeler, an Australian dingo-canine marriage bred to nip at the heels of wayward cattle to keep them in line. Whenever we take Bridget hiking, she runs loops around us, as if to herd us along according to some mysterious genetic dogma. The irony did not escape us that a dog tasked with corralling other creatures defied corralling herself. She has the speed of a cheetah and can accelerate from zero to sixty faster than a Mustang convertible. So being limited to the confines of a quasi-rural suburbia wasn't exactly to her liking.

We took to calling Bridget the *Pickup Truck Dog Living in the Minivan World*. Poor thing was ill suited to a universe not completely of her own free will. When the standard electric fence failed to restrain her escapist tendencies (I swear she sat there smugly buffing her nails, puffing her breath to polish them up just as she steeled herself for the breakout each time), we knew we had to graduate up to the "stubborn dog collar."

Powered by a nine-volt battery in a fist-sized pack, the collar issues a plentiful jolt to any border-crossing violator who dares compromise its perimeter. Finally we were able to somewhat confine Lulu to prevent her from being hit by a car (or terrifying elderly passersby and impressionable children with what ultimately became a rather menacing ice blue glare she'd mastered). We still recall the guilt-inducing moment at which Bridget first tried to breach her mother-of-all-dog-fences: She let out a yelp so long and loud that our parrot immediately picked it up and began repeating it, just to make us feel worse (even if it was for her own safety). This fence didn't always keep Lulu in; rather, it gave her pause to consider long and hard whether it was worth the zap. So at least her meanderings dropped from daily to quarterly. Progress, in our estimation.

The barking, however, seemed to defy any and all of our attempts to subdue it. We've been told it's the husky in her, but whatever it is, her barking is the hallmark and bane of our lives. Bridget barks to get in, she barks to go out, she barks to go up, she barks to come down. She barks to get fed, she barks because she doesn't want food. She barks at houseguests, our neighbors' houseguests, probably at houseguests in the neighborhood adjacent to ours. She barks at the mailman, the UPS man, the FedEx man. If we had a gardener, she'd bark at him (or her). She barks at people walking by, dogs walking by, cars driving by, birds flying by, bunnies hopping by, deer gamboling by, squirrels, mice, cats, tumbling leaves, mist, enveloping fog, fear-instilling thunder, jangling telephones, and our wing-flapping parrot. You name it, she barks at it.

Yes, attempts were made to curb the behavior. Clicker training—known to work even on feral cats!—meant to whip Bridget into obedience shape worked basically only when Bridget wanted it to. That would be when she was in the mood for the malodorous liver treats that worked best. Unfortunately, Bridget has always been an eat-to-live dog (unlike our live-to-eat Labrador, who would probably tap dance while whistling "Dixie" if it meant getting more food), and more often than not couldn't care less about a freebie Scooby Snack. Fact is, the only thing we had that she really wanted was her freedom.

And so one night when my husband was away and I was hosting a large gathering of women from the neighborhood for a ladies night out party, Bridget's barking became too much. Despite the deafening din of the chatter of nearly a hundred women, Bridget's shrill, ear-piercing bark each time the doorbell rang was threatening to ruin the party. Now, I know that everyone "in the know" in the dog world sees nothing wrong with crating a dog. Sure, crating has its purposes. But crating Bridget in particular always gave me pause, because despite her love of a good cave to protect her from an abiding fear of impending storms (trust me, she's crashed her way out of all containment vessels, scratched her way out of drywall and even wall-to-wall carpeting when the crack of thunder or fireworks is upon us), she loathed being stuffed in a dog crate. But I knew it might be my only chance at silencing the thing. I tried to placate her with a large beef bone.

Bridget had what's called a hard mouth and could chew her way through stainless steel if given enough time, so we'd abandoned cute little puppy toys—which ended in shreds and shards—in favor of the more durable beef shank bones, which I'd boil and stuff with cheese or peanut butter. I'm fairly certain hundreds of years hence, archaeologists will encounter countless cow femurs buried in the myriad holes that Bridget has dug in our once pristine yard and will wonder what kind of legs-only creature once must have roamed this land.

Sure enough, for the duration of the party, Bridget remained quiet in her spacious cage in the darkened mudroom. Somewhere in that reptilian area of my brain that senses impending disaster, I knew that she was stewing. Stewing and scheming. I just felt it in my bones. But a few glasses of wine later, I was sufficiently lubricated into a false level of trust in our little beastie girl.

A few weeks earlier I'd overheard a neighbor at a Christmas party lamenting, "And she just barks and barks and barks."

Still fairly new to our town, I was especially sensitive to our dog's intrusive ways.

"I hope you're not talking about Bridget," I said with more than a bit of trepidation.

"As a matter of fact, I am," she replied, minus any warm smile that would have assured me it was fine.

So when another invited neighbor couldn't attend my party because she had to awaken at four in the morning to catch a flight, I knew I didn't want Bridget to pull her usual shenanigans post-party and sneak out to bark at the moon and various nocturnal creatures when I wasn't looking.

Nearing midnight, as I focused my attention on hauling several leaking and bottle-laden garbage bags out the back door, that opportunistic canine, obscured from my view by the bags, thrust her way past my legs and took off into the night.

Dismayed, I at first stood on our back deck and naively tried kindness to coax Bridget into coming back into the house. Bridget, by then at the bottom of a steep seventy-degree hill that leads to our soccer-field-length backyard, was well beyond reach, and barking nonstop. Chasing the thing through land mines of dog poop and dug holes (her specialty) was not going to yield my prize. So I spoke with the mellifluous voice of a parent to a new-born, hoping cooler heads would prevail.

"Come on, sweetie," I cajoled.

Nothing.

"I'll give you a tre-at!" I promised, extending the word into two syllables.

If Bridget could have stuck up one paw and extended that middle digit my way, she would have. Instead she resumed her bark-a-thon.

After a good half hour of failed kindness, I tried wile. Maybe not SPCA-endorsed wile, but wile nonetheless. I went inside and picked up our aging, user-friendly calico cat, Hobbes, till then soundly sleeping on the sofa, and carried her out to the deck.

And then I did something I'm particularly not proud of: I held Hobbes aloft in a precursor to Michael Jackson on the balcony in Germany with his baby boy Blanket before his throng of adoring fans, and suspended the cat to tempt Bridget to come in. Okay, so I was tired. And I figured Bridget always loved a good cat bark session, so surely she'd fall for the old kitty-dangling maneuver, right?

But matching my exhausted-mom-of-three-and-four-glasses-of-wine-induced stupor to her perpetually alert wits was useless. Again came the one-finger salute. Figuratively, of course.

I then took to stewing in my *own* juices. By then a good hour had passed. It was after one in the morning; I was exhausted. My bark-averse neighbor was no doubt dialing the police to lodge a complaint. The other one was going to start her vacation exhausted and pissed at me. Since Bridget was nearly as fast as a gazelle, a chase would never land in the win column for me. What I needed, I knew, was a lasso. But I didn't have anything resembling that (nor the skills to use it).

Now understand, my brain was fogged. Logic was not at the forefront. But I remembered from obedience classes that a spray bottle of vinegar water works to stop bad behavior in dogs. Only she was far out of reach of my little spray bottle. But I remembered using a can of wasp spray one time and, damn, that stuff shot far. I picked up the phone, dialing the emergency vet.

"Hi," I said, warming up for the stupid question. "I was wondering, if I sprayed wasp spray at a dog just to temporarily disable her, would that endanger her?"

"Um, can I please have your name and address?" the vet tech asked.

Realizing that animal services would soon be two steps behind the police who were no doubt heading my way, I hung up. Okay, clearly wasp spray was toxic and a bad idea. But what? What could lure an intractable and deliberately defiant canine at what was then two in the morning? And then it came to me. In the dead of winter, on a frigid January night, while Bridget continued to bark undeterred, I fired up the gas grill and went inside to unearth a package of desiccated hot dogs buried in the bowels of my freezer. With a sharp knife and mallet, I hammered at the slab of rock-hard meat until two hot dogs gave way. And then I slapped those puppies on the grill.

I wondered if any neighbors noticed in their sleep the acute aroma of cooking hot dogs floating across the cold night air (and wonder what insane person was barbecuing at that hour). But I had my plan. And when the smell seemed to overtake even the hint of skunk that often lingers late at night, I knew it was time. I grabbed my frankfurters and proceeded down the steep hill to the flat yard.

"Hey, Bridge," I cooed.

"Look what I've got for yo-u!" I singsonged, knowing she was bullshit-proof but feeling desperate enough to give it a go anyway.

First she stopped barking for a minute. Then she brazenly made eye contact with me. I tried the "I'm the boss" stare, fixing my gaze upon hers with riveting intensity. Ever so slowly I inched forward, like a cop trying to persuade the bad guy to drop the gun. And I dangled those weenies, closer and closer. *Promise, I'll get the judge to reduce your sentence if you just come willingly.*

And finally, *whomp!* Straight out of the fairy tale in which the fox chomps down on the Gingerbread Man, Bridget made her move, snatching at one of the hot dogs in a front-back pivot attempt to grab and go. But I was pissed, and a defiant dog is no match for an angry, exhausted me in the middle of the night. I reached down, grabbed her collar, and marched her up the hill without benefit of a hot dog reward, which I flung in the woods for some other wild creature to enjoy, while strains from the ebullient victory march in *Peter and the Wolf* played in my mind.

Over the years, Bridget has mellowed. And despite the frustrations with her defiance, we love our girl and appreciate that much of her dominance, at least in her mind, is for our own good: She's got our backs, even if it means she's not exactly in close proximity while she has them.

I've always felt bad that we didn't have the time to channel Bridget's energies by training her with canine agility classes, or even dog Frisbee. She was ready-made for such fun. But the other side of that is she's had a long, happy, and somewhat independent life with us. Had we not rescued her, or had she been adopted by someone who then listened to the advice and got rid of her, Bridget would never have lived to see a decade of life, because she would have been put down.

As she climbs into her twilight years, she can't always run like she used to. Two torn ACLs keep her down occasionally, rendering her a bit like a thoroughbred left to pasture. But sometimes she'll muster up the same eff-you attitude she used to use with the stubborn dog fence and will spring into action to chase some deer or a rabbit. Her hard mouth has become softer; bad dental genes have left her with a tooth deficit. And the older she gets, the more she is hamstrung by impending storms (some internal barometer of hers has always warned her hours beforehand). But Bridget has remained loyal and loving and every day we are so grateful we didn't listen to that well-intended advice to get rid of our adorable little pooch. She's enriched our lives probably more than we hers, and even when she is gone she will be immortalized for the rest of Graycie's life each time the parrot warns our Smoochie girl not to eat her by saying, "Bridget, no! You're a bad, bad girl!"

Are You Smarter Than a Terrier?

Beth Kendrick

I picked out Murphy the way I imagine a socially stunted middle-aged man might select an Eastern European mail-order bride: late at night, hopped up on processed snack foods, guided only by an Internet profile featuring a few grainy photos and a paragraph of personal history.

But I didn't need a bunch of nitty-gritty details. One look and I knew—I'd found my soul mate.

"Look at this one." I called my husband over to check out the listing on Petfinder.com. "Look at that darling little face! And those ears. We were meant to be—I can feel it."

"Are you sure you wouldn't rather get a goldfish?" He barely glanced at the flickering picture of the scruffy terrier mix who bore a striking resemblance to Max from *How the Grinch Stole Christmas*. "Maybe a nice hermit crab?"

I didn't dignify that with a response. Larry and I had gotten married three months earlier, and before we walked down the aisle, we'd hammered out a verbal prenup: I would start rooting for the New York Jets, and he would agree to adopt the dog of my choosing. (Full disclosure: I'm still a Bears fan. But I didn't tell him that until after we were up to three dogs.)

So I e-mailed the rescue group to initiate the adoption screening process. Although Larry and I were novice dog owners, it weighed heavily in our favor that we were in the process of moving from an apartment in Los Angeles to a single-family house in Phoenix, where we would be able to offer Murphy a fenced yard, grassy neighborhood parks, and a slavishly devoted owner who worked from home. After a quick meet and greet, the cofounder of the rescue group approved our application. He also told us how Murphy had ended up in the rescue group: The poor little mongrel had been found wandering the streets of South Central L.A., filthy, starving, but possessing an unmistakable charm and charisma. Oliver Twist with fur and fleas. Our hearts melted. We wrote the check, signed the contract, and picked up our new pack member on our way out of town.

Murphy didn't say much on the six-hour drive to Arizona. He curled up in the backseat, his gaze melancholy, and seemed reluctant to exit the car for walks when we stopped for gas. He turned up his nose at the premium kibble I offered him, to the point that I started to worry.

"What if he's sick?" I asked Larry as we pulled up to the In-N-Out drive-through. "What if he's so heartbroken to leave the only home he's ever known that he literally dies of the anguish?"

That's when Murphy caught a whiff of my husband's burger, and suddenly, a spark of life appeared in his liquid brown eyes. We offered him a broiled beef patty and he devoured it, then licked our hands to make sure he'd ingested every last molecule of meat.

I would later look back and pinpoint this moment as the opening salvo in his coup d'etat.

Despite his rakish good looks, this dog was no dumb blond.

He was Niccolo Machiavelli trapped in Benji's body, and his campaign for world domination started with the hamburger, then progressed to the sleeping arrangements.

Before Larry and I finalized Murphy's adoption, we agreed on one very important ground rule: The dog would not sleep in our bed. The dog could sleep *next* to our bed, in a crate or a cushy nest of blankets, but not *in* the bed. We were newlyweds, and our bed was our sacred sanctuary. End of discussion.

We arrived in Phoenix on New Year's Day, which meant that the city's utility service offices were closed for the holiday, which meant that our new house did not yet have electricity or hot water. So we checked into a pet-friendly hotel, collapsed into bed, and turned off the lights.

That's when the barking started. Murphy, who up 'til now had not uttered so much as a whimper, let loose with a string of high-pitched barks that set my teeth on edge.

"Oh my God," Larry said. "I'm deaf."

"I will handle this," I announced.

I turned on the lights, led Murphy gently but firmly back to his pimped-out orthopedic dog bed, commanded him to stay, and snuggled back under the covers.

This shut him up for all of two seconds. Then he started barking again, even louder.

"Just ignore him," I whispered. "He has to learn that we mean what we say."

Rowf, rowf, rowf.

"This hotel is booked to capacity and the walls are paper-thin," Larry said.

"Trust me—ignore him. I took a whole class on animal cognition in grad school. I know whereof I speak."

223

ROWF! ROWF! ROWF!

Our next-door neighbor pounded on the wall.

"I am not sleeping in the car tonight," Larry said. "Let him up on the foot of the bed. Just this once."

And with that, all our ground rules went straight out the window, along with a semester's worth of animal cognition. Murphy nestled into the crook behind my knees, suddenly sleepy and serene.

"Don't get too comfortable," I warned him. "This will never happen again."

Two days later, I took Murphy to the vet for a checkup. He capered around the waiting room, begging for treats and glad-handing the receptionists. Then the exam got under way and there were a lot of sidelong glances and scribbling in the chart.

"What?" I kept asking the tech, who refused to make eye contact. "What?"

Turned out, Murphy must have had an owner at some point during his hardscrabble upbringing on the south side. In addition to a D.I.Y. docked tail, he had matching ear hematomas, indicating that someone had cropped his ears in a less than humane fashion. But that was not the reason for all the chart scribbling.

Several hundred dollars and many X-rays later, the vet broke the bad news: "Your dog has a broken hip." She clipped a black-and-white scan to the light box. "Actually, his whole pelvis is shattered. It looks like he got hit by a car."

I gaped at her, openmouthed.

She lifted one eyebrow. "You had no idea?"

In the few days we'd known him, Murphy never betrayed his injury with the slightest limp. He raced after birds at the park with speed that put greyhounds to shame. He had a vertical leap like

Michael Jordan and could snatch a used Kleenex out of my hand midair. When we called the rescue group to report all this, they were just as shocked as we were.

The vet referred us to a surgeon, who opened up Murphy's hip, and declared, "It looks like a jigsaw puzzle in there," but did the best she could to realign what was left of his pelvic girdle and scrape out loose bone chips along with years' worth of scar tissue. While he was recovering from surgery, he had many fresh incisions and several types of pain medications, and to ensure that he didn't chew out his stitches or hurt himself while loopy on opiates, we let him sleep on the bed again, "just for a few more days."

Over the next few months, I took him to a series of orthopedic specialists and drove across the city twice weekly for canine physical therapy sessions. We experimented with grain-free diets and fish oil supplements to reduce tissue inflammation. But let's be real, there's only so much you can do to cobble together a thousand shattered shards of skeleton. Murphy's body was never going to be whole again, but in true terrier fashion, he figured out a way to work this to his advantage. At home, his injury remained undetectable to the naked eye. When we were out and about, however, and strangers exclaimed over how adorable he was, Murphy would start hobbling around with an exaggerated limp and martyred-saint eyes. His new acquaintances would immediately shower him with affection and whatever food they happened to have on them, and he would accept all this with a thumping tail stub and a brave show of stoicism in the aftermath of tragedy. Then the suckers would continue on their way and Murphy would resume strutting along like Gisele on the catwalk.

A year or so after we adopted Murphy, I had another late-night snack-food episode on Petfinder, and we ended up with two large, lovable red mutts. Roxie Hart (What can I say? The dog has stage presence) is a doe-eyed little lady so sweet that I ended up training her to be a therapy dog at a family crisis shelter. Friday is a wrinkly browed lug with jaws like an alligator, a head like an anvil, and only two states of consciousness: comatose and semi-comatose. Both of them outweighed Murphy by at least forty pounds, yet he ruled over them with an iron fist, treating them like fraternity pledges in a never-ending Hell Week. When he wasn't ordering his oversized flunkies to fetch him bonbons or shaking them down for their Nylabones, he was tattling on them for the slightest infractions.

"That Murphy's something else," my mom said when she came out to Phoenix for a visit. Apparently, she'd left an empty plastic water bottle on our coffee table and Roxie, unable to resist anything that might conceivably serve as a chew toy, had nabbed it and smuggled it out the doggie door into the backyard. Murphy immediately launched into his trademark bark, and when no one rushed out to punish Roxie, he wrestled the water bottle away from her, carried it back inside, and dropped it at my mother's feet. "He's like Lassie."

Exactly like Lassie. Except, rather than wasting his time with some snot-nosed kid trapped in a well, Murphy reserved his vigilance for catching his subordinates in the act of counter-surfing, a crime he believed should be punishable by forfeiture of dinner and/or death.

It goes without saying that Roxie and Friday were banned from the bed. Hell, Larry and I were lucky to be up there at this point. Over the years, Murphy had expanded his personal mattress territory by snuggling into the valley of comforter between me and my husband, then bracing his back against me, his feet against Larry, and slooowly stretching out his legs and locking his knees. Blanketless, we shivered and clung to the edges, sleeping fitfully between bouts of canine kickboxing and snoring. We had long ago given up on evicting him, so our only revenge was humiliation and cheap laughs. I would drape a sheet over his head, kerchief-style, and pretend he was an old-timey Russian peasant waiting in the bread line. We had a little voice for him and everything: "Alms for the poor."

Every night after dinner, we would torment him by grabbing his leash, twirling it around, and making him wait for us to drop the W-word. Larry would casually remark, "Hey, Beth, I was thinking about doing some painting. Have you seen my *smock*?"

To which I would reply, "No, but I'm going to the pawnshop later, so let me know if you've got anything to *hock*."

"What time is it? Let me check the *clock*."

We would go through endless variations—*sock, Glock, dock, rock*—before finally acknowledging the irate yellow dog waiting by the door: "Oh, gosh, Murphy, I didn't see you there. Did you happen to want a *walk*?"

We cracked ourselves up.

Murphy knew he was being *mock*ed, and he'd glare at us with blistering scorn, clearly praying for the power of speech so he could deliver to us the verbal flaying we deserved, but he bided his time and took his revenge when he knew it would hurt us most—the crack of dawn on Sunday morning.

With the unerring precision of a fine Swiss timepiece, Murphy demanded breakfast at six thirty a.m. sharp every morning. Six thirty-one was unacceptable. Weekends and holidays were no excuse. So every day, at exactly six twenty-nine, he would crouch over Larry, fix him with psycho, spirally eyes, and emit a series of little half woofs. He knew that full-fledged barking was forbidden, so instead of busting out the full *rowf*, he'd just go *rrr*—(pause), *ro*—(pause), *row*—until Larry opened one eye just a crack. This was Murphy's cue to drape himself across Larry's face and start wagging his entire body, which would whip Roxie and Friday into a frenzy. The master bedroom devolved into a canine tornado of whining, slobbering, and shedding until somebody broke down and coughed up some kibble.

Because Murphy had beaten so many odds over the years, I let myself believe that his devastating injuries would never catch up with him. He was sassy and spry, and I had every confidence that he could single-handedly pioneer the necessary stem cell/reparative gene therapy to rebuild his skeletal structure when his pelvic bones finally gave out. But then, one rainy autumn evening, he started limping for real. Not to score food or attention, but because crippling arthritis had set in. He stopped hogging the bed at night and started sleeping with his hip pressed against my belly, using me as a human heating pad. Our vet upped the dosage of his anti-inflammatory and prescribed heavy-duty painkillers, but nothing helped. He started going after the other dogs when they accidentally jostled him, not with warning nips but with real bites. We knew it was time to let him go when the diabolical glint in his eyes dimmed and we had to start coaxing him to start his day at the unheard-of hour of eight a.m.

Putting Murphy down was one of the hardest decisions I've ever made; although his body could no longer function, his mind remained razor-sharp. Larry offered to take him to the vet's office for the last time, but we both understood that in all the ways that mattered most, Murphy was mine. I had to see him all the way through.

I wish I could say that I displayed the same unflinching terrier toughness that Murphy did when his final moments arrived, but I was a blotchy-eyed, runny-nosed, ugly crying mess. "We're never getting another dog," I told Larry between sobs. "I can't go through this again."

Two weeks later, my Web browser found itself open to Petfinder.com.

I'll always love Murphy and I'll never forget him—not that I could, he made sure of that. To this day, we find errant wisps of his yellow fur lodged in the back of the linen closet and deep in the bowels of the couch. A pointed reminder, across space and time and the sweet hereafter, that he will always be my scruffy-eared soul mate . . . and he's got first dibs on the bed forever.

Fairy Tales Can Come True

Jill Conner Browne

Ever take notice of how quickly your life can change forever? One minute you're just bumbling along as usual and then, without the slightest suspicion on your part that *something* is about to happen that will put a Major Wrinkle in your existence, suddenly you feel metal underfoot and too late you realize that you have just stepped on the garden hoe and the knowledge that you are about to be struck smack in the middle of the face with the handle traveling at warp speed comes just a nanosecond too late for you to dodge it. Sometimes, it's a tragedy—sometimes, it's a glorious gift—sometimes, it's not what you think it is at all, even when it's happening. Life sometimes sends out previews—but It never reveals the Surprise Ending.

This story is so amazing you might expect it to begin with "Once upon a time, long long ago." But it's *true*, so it goes like this: I am driving to the YMCA at about nine a.m. to teach an aerobics class. As I approach the Woodrow Wilson Overpass, I have just the slightest sense of foreboding. Traffic is not behaving very well. As I come closer, I see, to my utter amazement, that there is a *pack of dogs*—on the interstate bridge, circulating freely among the traffic. As I inch closer, I see that one of the dogs has been hit, and she is dragging herself by her front legs, trying desperately to get out of the road, but alas, *none* of the sonsabitches in the cars will stop long enough to let her get past.

If I live to be a hundred, I will never forget the look on that dog's face as she struggled so frantically to save herself.

I stopped my car—right in the middle of the interstate bridge—and got out. I walked over to the injured pooch and spoke softly to her. Incredibly, she allowed me to pick her up without the slightest struggle or whimper. She was quite an armful, and as I made my way to the back of my station wagon, I realized I had an upcoming dilemma: how to open the hatch while cradling this large wounded dog? It was clearly not doable solo. I turned to look at the drivers of the now stopped vehicles behind me until one of them slipped up and made eye contact. If eyeballs could grasp, then mine performed the equivalent of reaching through her car window and hauling her out by the nape of the neck and demanding that she *Get over here and open this door for me, you miserable wretch*, which she meekly did. I thanked her profusely, just as if she had done it willingly and with a glad heart, even though we both knew differently. She slunk back to her car. I climbed in mine and made haste to the nearest vet's office.

Bursting into the doctor's office, exclaiming that I had just rescued this injured dog from the middle of a highway bridge, I and my victim were able to cut in line ahead of any number of well-coiffed Shih Tzus and assorted other glamorous, pampered pets and their humans. The staff scrambled as if I were bringing in the Pope on a gurney, and indeed, I doubt whether the Pope himself has ever been as gently and lovingly addressed and treated. It was determined that there was a hairline fracture in the dog's pelvis and she was going to need some hospital time.

I was fine throughout this ordeal until I got into my car to leave and then . . . I just lost it. Calling my erstwhile husband, formerly known as MoonPie (more recently known by Other Names so let's just stick with that one), I managed to gulp and sob out the whole story of the rescue—every time I thought of her terrified little face, a new wave of bawling would ensue; so, it took some few minutes to relay the details of my morning, which concluded with the declaration that, in private conversation with the dog on the way to the vet, I had promised her that if she would just hang on and get well, she could live with us. This last part was met with utter silence on the other end of the line, especially when the dog's pedigree was revealed as "brown and sorta fat." That silence, however, was met with an even more powerful commitment on my end.

First of all, my People have a long, well-documented love affair with Brown Dogs (fat and otherwise), but furthermore, I had made a promise to a dog and I would not break it. Although it should be avoided, you *can* break promises to people if you *have* to—because you can explain circumstances and make reasonable justifications and compromises with people. *Dogs take you at your word*—that's a lot to live up to—and I, for one, do not want to *be* the kind of person who reneges on a good-faith deal with a dog. You think Karma doesn't have a dog? I'll take that bet all day long.

Needless to say, this particular brown dog was released into my loving custody a few days later, but our path was not to be a smooth one. First of all, I had to set her down on my front porch to unlock the door—only to have my eardrums torn asunder by the alarm on the security system that MoonPie had for unknowable reasons chosen to set for the first time ever, without advising me of same. Cursing him, I managed to turn the thing off (making a mental note to set it off that night right as he was drifting off to sleep, just for grins), and looked around to see a brown blur hurtling down the street, with no trace of a limp.

At this point, the brown dog had not even been *given* a name, let alone had time to learn and respond to it, so all I could do was lope off after her. Suffice it to say that even a dog with a broken pelvis could outrun me, and this one did—all the way to one of the busiest four-lane roads in our whole city.

By the time I caught up, somehow, she had made it across two lanes of traffic to the median, while I was stuck on the sidewalk. As difficult as it might be to communicate *"Come back"* to a dog with whom one is barely acquainted, let me assure you that *"Stay"* is just a waste of time and breath.

Having fled my home, run from me and all my most heartfelt entreaties, and only now pausing to consider the potential ramifications of her choices, the brown dog looked across the sea of racing automobiles and seemed to decide, "Eh, what the hell—where else am I gonna go?" and she tentatively put one brown paw down onto the traffic lane as I resorted to mindless shrieking from my side of the street.

The drivers in the lane closest to me were clearly of superior intelligence, as luck would have it, and they had observed the scenario unfolding before them and made the wise and compassionate choice to stop as I ran out in front of them—but the jackass in the big ole Lincoln in the far lane—the one now containing that one delicately placed brown paw—showed no such kindly inclination. Perhaps I judge him harshly and mistakenly. It is, I suppose, possible that he was one of your rare *blind* drivers and thus truly did not see all six feet one inch of me, lumbering across the road, with my hands literally outstretched and clasped in an attitude of *begging* in his general direction. Perhaps he was also hearing-impaired and thus his ears were spared the sounds of my caterwauling being inflicted on the auditory canals of all others within a mile or so. Or perhaps he was, in fact, just your garden-variety jackass. Whatever. I knew if he hit *my* ass, it was gonna total the front end of that Lincoln, and I made the snap judgment that he was prolly underinsured for collision, not to mention short of bail money, so if he wanted to play chicken, he picked the wrong opponent.

The brown dog again allowed me to scoop her up out of traffic, but this time she showed her enthusiasm by peeing all over both of us. So, I trudged home, urine-soaked, carrying my prize. After cleaning us both up, I made her a bed in my daughter Bailey's bathroom, and after some soothing snacks and conversation, I left her alone to rest and collect her thoughts.

When Bailey came home from school, I advised her of our new family member and told her not to go in there without me, explaining the overwhelming events of the afternoon and stressing the need for solitude and peace. Bailey, six at the time, grasped this theory instantly and was in complete agreement and compliance.

Somewhat later, the erstwhile husband made his eventual return home and, big surprise, ignored all my explanations and instructions, barged straight into the bathroom, flipping on all the lights and speaking too loudly, and promptly got himself a dog bite. He launched immediately into all manner of proclamations about the actions and future fate of the brown dog—all of which fell on ears that were not so much deaf as *outraged*!

I informed *him* that what we had here is a dog who has been lost, run over, rescued from a bridge, spent a week in a hospital, been sent home with a stranger, had a 900-decibel alarm go off in her face, run two miles on a broken pelvis, played in traffic *again*, was rescued by the same woman, and had *just* got settled down for a nap when some *guy* she's never seen before comes busting up in *her new home*.

I told him I thought the brown dog made the best decision possible, based on the information available to her at the time—biting the shit outta him—and I freely admitted to feeling a similar inclination myownself at the moment—and hardly for the first time. Furthermore, I told him, *the dog* would be *staying*; he, on the other hand, could certainly make his own choice and best of luck with that.

MoonPie eventually made peace with the brown dog and so he was allowed to stay . . . for a bit longer. Although it must be told that the brown dog, superior being that she was, made the first overture. I had spoken to her frankly about her animosity toward him—and allowed as how I could totally understand where she was coming from, but I asked her if, as a personal favor to me, she would consider some sort of conciliatory act toward him, in the interest of domestic tranquillity. After a few hours' thought on the matter, she came into the room where MoonPie was lying on the floor, staring at a NASCAR race on TV. Giving me a look that spoke volumes, she sighed and walked over to him, stretched out on her side, and extended one little brown paw toward him. Harder hearts than his have been melted by less and all was made well—once again, through the wordless but boundlessly articulate communication of a dog.

The brown dog was very much in need of a name, though,

and, as it happened, I already had a couple in mind. Six years earlier, when we learned that we would be having a precious baby girl, we spent the whole nine months it took to hatch her pondering on names. The day she was born, I knew at once who she was and named her for two of the dearest women in all of my life. Shortly after the birth and naming of our precious baby girl, MoonPie's best friend, one "Pete" from Atlanta, acquired himself a puppy—to which he assigned the *very same name* as our *daughter*. And thus, when we found ourselves in possession of a new dog of the female persuasion, needing a name, I told MoonPie that *he* could choose . . . with one caveat: "Pete" had himself a wife and a daughter, both with perfectly acceptable girl-type names, either of which would be suitable for *our* dog. He could choose between "Sharon" and "Jena." And so, the days rolled by and Sharon became part of our family, getting along easily with our other dogs, the cats, and even the erstwhile husband.

By and by, regular checkup time rolled around for our other dogs, which offered the perfect time for Sharon to be introduced to our family vet. Boy, were we in for a surprise. No sooner had we walked in the door with our four-legged posse than we were set upon by every doctor and staff member in the office with gleeful shouts of *"Poochie-Mama! It's Poochie-Mama! Omigod! It's a miracle! Poochie-Mama is here!"*

Nonplussed would not begin to cover it for us. Self-centered as the day is long, of course, I initially think they're talking about *me*, and I'm less than thrilled at being referred to as *any* kind of "mama" by any group of people other than those to whom I may have personally given birth, and *"Poochie"* would, of course, be unacceptable, coming from any source that wanted to continue breathing air. It took a minute or so to realize that they were referring to *Sharon* and to realize that they knew her from her Former Days, before she hit the road, as it were, and before it hit her back.

One of the vets finally managed to rein in her Poochie-Mama-induced hysteria long enough to begin telling us the Story—but as she was telling it, the receptionist was on the phone, calling Poochie-Mama's mama, and when that connection was made and the news of Poochie-Mama's Miraculous Appearance was delivered, the whole room erupted into great whooping shouts of joy and huge buckets of happy tears were shed.

Well, it seems that Poochie-Mama's mama, Linda, had cancer—a big bad one, and she had to go way, far off, for a long time, for a bone marrow transplant. Poochie-Mama was a one-woman dog and she had gone into mourning over Linda's absence—which, of course, could not be satisfactorily explained to her, her being a dog and all, and after a while, she just decided to take matters into her own paws and she set off on a search for Linda, which didn't get any farther than that interstate bridge.

Meanwhile, Linda was in total isolation because of the bone marrow transplant. She had one sacred ritual performed daily, with almost religious fervor, to hold on to some semblance of normalcy and sanity: Late every afternoon, at about the time in "real life" when she should have been getting home from the office, she would lie in her hospital bed and softly call out for her dog, "Pooooochie-Mama! Mama's home! Come here, girl! Poooooochie-Mama!" And in her mind, Linda could hear the tap-tap-tap of the brown dog's toenails on the driveway as she ran up in happy greeting. She would imagine fondling Poochie-Mama's silky ears and rubbing her fat belly, which would quickly be presented for that very purpose.

I believe that, in the mysterious realm of Dog Omnipotence,

Poochie-Mama heard Linda's call, followed it miles to the interstate, and had her journey not been so rudely interrupted by her injury I have no doubt that she would have eventually walked into Linda's hospital room, road-weary but very happy to have found her Woman at last.

Obviously, while Linda was literally fighting for her life, nobody could bring themselves to tell her that Poochie-Mama had gone missing, and so, even though her eventual homecoming was an ecstatic time for her and her whole family—we can't really even imagine her sadness when there was no tap-tap of toenails, no silky ears, no fat, furry belly to rub, no Poochie-Mama there to share the joy of that homecoming, that she had unknowingly done so much to help make possible.

For Linda, days turned into weeks, weeks to months—and her gratitude and happiness with being home were always tempered by her grief at the loss of the one blessed creature that had helped her survive. (Isn't that just the sum of Dogs right there—how they help us and heal us without even knowing it?) And then, one random afternoon, no different from any other, her phone rings and there's a crazy-happy person on the other end, telling her, *"Poochie-Mama's been found!"*

And they lived happily ever after. (Cue orchestra and choir of angels.)

Contributor Bios

Or, What We Do When We're Not
Walking You, Feeding You, Petting You,
Grooming You, or Cleaning Up After You

Alice Bradley

Alice Bradley writes Finslippy (www.finslippy.com), a personal blog, and cowrites Let's Panic About Babies! (www.lets-panic .com), a fake parenting site. *Let's Panic About Babies!*, the book, was just published by St. Martin's Press in the spring of 2011. Alice's work has been featured in numerous anthologies, magazines, and Web sites, including *Redbook*, Nerve, the *Sun*, the Onion News Network, and Fence. She was nominated for a Pushcart Prize in nonfiction. Alice lives in Brooklyn with her husband, son, dog, and cat. Alice supports the Brooklyn Animal Resource Coalition (BARC; www.barcshelter.org/).

Jill Conner Browne

Multiple #1 *New York Times* bestselling author Jill Conner Browne, THE Sweet Potato Queen™, has created a global phenomenon— six thousand chapter groups in twenty-two countries—based upon her philosophy and worldview as recounted through her rollicking, raucous, and riotously funny essays. Women and smart men understand that the bawdy, sassy, down-to-earth humor is simply the vehicle by which the greater message is conveyed— that is, one of self-reliance and empowerment, inspiring all to do what makes their hearts sing. For more, visit www.sweetpotato queens.com/. Jill supports the Animal Rescue Fund of Mississippi (www.arfms.com); ARF was founded by one of Jill's actual Sweet Potato Queens®, "Pippa" Jackson, who wears the official SPQ out-fit and rides on Jill's float in the annual parade.

Rita Mae Brown

Rita Mae Brown is the *New York Times* bestselling author of the Mrs. Murphy mystery series (which she writes with her tiger cat, Sneaky Pie) and the Sister Jane novels, as well as *Rubyfruit Jungle*, *In Her Day*, *Six of One*, *The Sand Castle*, and the memoirs *Animal Magnetism* and *Rita Will*. An Emmy-nominated screenwriter and a poet, Brown lives in Afton, Virginia, with cats, hounds, horses, and big red foxes. For more, visit www.ritamaebrown.com. Rita Mae founded the Almost Home Pet Adoption Center, a no-kill shelter in Virginia (www.nelsonspca.org/).

W. Bruce Cameron

W. Bruce Cameron is an internationally syndicated humor columnist who has twice been voted Best Humor Columnist by the National Society of Newspaper Columnists and has won the Robert Benchley award for humor. In June 2011 he was voted Columnist of the Year at the National Columnist convention in Detroit. His book *8 Simple Rules for Dating My Teenage Daughter* was developed into the TV series *8 Simple Rules*, starring the late John Ritter. His most recent novel, *A Dog's Purpose*, was a *New York Times* bestselling book, a *USA Today* bestseller, and a *Los Angeles Times* bestseller. *A Dog's Purpose* is being developed as a motion picture by DreamWorks. His new novel, *Emory's Gift*, was published in August by Forge. For more, visit www.brucecameron.com. Bruce supports the Life Is Better Rescue, an animal rescue charity (lifeisbetterrescue.org).

Caprice Crane

Caprice Crane is the internationally bestselling author of four novels and a writer for both television and screen. Her newest novel, *With a Little Luck*, hit shelves in the summer of 2011, well timed with the release of her first feature film, *Love Wedding Marriage*, starring Mandy Moore and Kellan Lutz. Her recent past included staff positions writing for hit TV shows, such as *90210* (2.0) and the revamped *Melrose Place*. Crane currently divides her time between New York and Los Angeles, depending on the mood of her dog, Max. Her Web site is www.capricecrane.com. Caprice supports the Toby Project (www.tobyproject.org/).

Jenny Gardiner

Jenny Gardiner is the author of the award-winning novel *Sleeping with Ward Cleaver*, *Winging It: A Memoir of Caring for a Vengeful Parrot Who's Determined to Kill Me*, *Slim to None* and *Over the Falls*. Her work has been found in *Ladies' Home Journal*, in the *Washington Post*, and on NPR's *Day to Day*. She and her family live in Virginia with a slew of pets that rule the roost. Visit her at her Web site, www.jennygardiner.net. Jenny supports the Charlottesville-Albemarle SPCA, a no-kill shelter (www.caspca.org/).

Jane Green

Jane Green Warburg is the author of twelve novels, including the bestselling *Jemima J.*, *The Beach House*, and *Promises to Keep*. A former journalist, she writes a daily blog at www.janegreen.com and contributes to various publications, including the *Sunday*

Times, Huffington Post, Wowowow.com, and *Self*. A foodie and passionate cook, she lives in Connecticut with her husband, six children, and more animals than she can really handle. Jane supports the Connecticut Humane Society (www.cthumane.org).

Annabelle Gurwitch

The actress and writer Annabelle Gurwitch's most recent book, *You Say Tomato, I Say Shut Up: A Love Story*, published by Crown in 2010, is a comedic memoir cowritten with her Emmy Award–winning comedy writer husband, Jeff Kahn. Her first book, *Fired: Tales of the Canned, Canceled, Downsized and Dismissed*, is a comedic look at being made redundant. Her acting credits include *Dinner and a Movie* and *Seinfeld*; she was a commentator for numerous years on NPR; her essays also appear in the anthologies *Note to Self* and *Rejected!* Failure and humiliation seem to be her oeuvre. For more, visit www.annabellegurwitch.com. Annabelle supports Tails of Joy! (www.tailsofjoy.net/).

Chunk Handler, Foreword

I'm Chelsea Handler's dog. Follow me on Twitter (twitter.com/chunkhandler) or Facebook, or at my mom's Web site, www.chelseahandler.com. I was adopted from the West Los Angeles Animal Shelter.

Beth Harbison

Beth Harbison is the *New York Times* bestselling author of *Shoe Addicts Anonymous*, *Hope in a Jar*, and *Always Something There to*

Remind Me. She is a dog lover from way back, though she usually likes one of her dogs better than the other. Fortunately, it's usually the one everyone else likes less. She lives near Washington, D.C., in a house that looks like the one in *Lady and the Tramp.* More info can be found about her at BethHarbison.com. Beth supports Pet-Connect (petconnectrescue.org).

Beth Kendrick

Beth Kendrick is the author of *The Bake-Off, Second Time Around,* and five other novels. She has a Ph.D. in psychology, which in no way prepared her to match wits with a terrier. She lives with her family in Arizona, where her husband has blocked her computer access to Petfinder.com. For more information, please visit her Web site at www.BethKendrick.com. Beth supports Tucson Cold Wet Noses (www.tucsoncoldwetnoses.com).

Stephanie Klein

The internationally acclaimed author of the memoirs *Straight Up and Dirty* and *Moose: A Memoir of Fat Camp,* Klein (stephanieklein .com) is one of the Internet's most popular icons. While currently developing her work for TV and film, she's completing her latest memoir, *When the Cookie Crumbles,* about how her downright grueling experiences as a leader in the Girl Scouts of the USA have saved her marriage, friendships, and life. Stephanie supports Austin Pets Alive! (www.austinpetsalive.org).

Jen Lancaster

Jen Lancaster is the *New York Times* bestselling author of *If You Were Here*; *My Fair Lazy*; *Pretty in Plaid*; *Such a Pretty Fat*; *Bright Lights, Big Ass*; and *Bitter Is the New Black*. A nationally syndicated monthly columnist for Tribune Media Services' Humor Hotel, she lives in Chicago. Visit her blog at www.jennsylvania.com. Jen supports Save-A-Pet (www.saveapetil.org/index.php).

Allie Larkin

Allie Larkin lives in Rochester, New York, with her husband, Jeremy, their two German shepherds, Argo and Stella, and a three-legged cat. She is the cofounder of TheGreenists.com, a site dedicated to helping readers take simple steps toward going green, and blogs at AllieLarkinWrites.com. Her first novel, *Stay* (published by Dutton in 2010), is about love, friendship, and a German shepherd named Joe. Allie supports Wooftown Rescue, Inc. (http://www.wooftowndoggydaycare.com/adopt_a_dog).

Alec Mapa

Alec Mapa is an internationally beloved actor and comedian. Alec has had starring roles on *Desperate Housewives* and *Ugly Betty* and has appeared in the films *You Don't Mess With the Zohan*, *Marley and Me*, and *Connie and Carla*. He is the host of the daily syndicated talk show *Gossip Queens*, and lives in Los Angeles with his husband, Jamie, their son, Zion, and two dogs, Ozzy and Sweet Pea. For more, please visit www.alecmapa.com. Alec supports the North Central Los Angeles Shelter, "The best place

in LA to meet a new friend!" (www.laanimalservices.com/nc_
carecenter.htm).

Jeff Marx

Jeff Marx is an ex-lawyer who cocreated and cowrote the music
and lyrics for the Tony Award–winning hit Broadway musical *Avenue Q*. Jeff supports Los Angeles Animal Services (www.laanimal
services.com/).

Laurie Notaro

Laurie Notaro is the author of a bunch of *New York Times* bestselling books, including *The Idiot Girls' Action-Adventure Club* and
Spooky Little Girl, and met Maeby at the local dog pound. They live
in Eugene, Oregon, where Maeby hogs the bed and freely farts.
Maeby is currently at work on a riveting screenplay about her experiences protecting her kingdom from noisy yet unseen things in
the alley. For more, visit www.laurienotaro.com. Laurie supports
Greenhill Humane Society, a no-kill shelter (www.green-hill.org/).

Sarah Pekkanen

Sarah Pekkanen is the author of the hit novels *The Opposite of Me*,
which has been translated into five languages, and *Skipping a Beat*,
which was published in February 2011 by Washington Square
Press, an imprint of Simon & Schuster, Inc. Sarah is an award-winning former journalist whose work has appeared on NPR's *All
Things Considered* and in publications including *People* magazine
and the *Washington Post*. She lives in Chevy Chase, Maryland, with

her husband, three young sons, and rescue Lab Bella. Please visit her Web site at www.sarahpekkanen.com or find her on Facebook. And for the Web site that introduced Bella to Sarah, visit www.lab-rescue.com.

Eddie Sarfaty

The comedian and writer Eddie Sarfaty has appeared on the *Today* show, Comedy Central's *Premium Blend*, and Logo's *Wisecrack*, and is a subject of the documentary *Laughing Matters*. He is the author of a book of humorous essays entitled *Mental: Funny in the Head* (Kensington, 2009), and is on the faculty of the Theatre Lab in Washington, D.C., and New York University, where he teaches courses in stand-up and comedy writing. Eddie can be found online at www.KeepLaughing.com. Eddie supports Guide Dogs for the Blind (www.guidedogs.com).

Bob Smith

Bob Smith is the author of the bestselling humorous memoirs *Openly Bob* (winner of a Lambda Literary Award) and *Way to Go, Smith*. His first novel, *Selfish and Perverse*, was one of three nominees for the Edmund White Award for Debut Fiction, and his most recent book is the novel *Remembrance of Things I Forgot*. As a stand-up comic, he broke barriers as the first openly gay comedian to appear on the *Tonight Show* and was featured in his own HBO comedy special. His comic essays and articles have appeared in the *Advocate* and *Out*. He grew up in Buffalo, New York, and lives in New York City. For more, visit www.literati.net/Smith or e-mail Bob at bobscomedy@aol.com. Bob supports Broadway Barks (www.broadwaybarks.com).

A Note from the Editor

My life, like most of you reading this anthology, has been defined by dogs. I've had six dogs in my life, and each was as different from the other as a brother from a sister. But all had this in common: All were rescues who loved me unconditionally, and taught me to love and laugh without limit.

My mother was a lifelong nurse, who—in her retirement—became a hospice nurse. Her entire life was spent caring for others, nurturing not only their health but also their spirit. That included animals in our rural Ozarks town: cats and dogs who were routinely abandoned, abused and dumped along dirt roads, or in our woods. She tried to save every single one, using heavy doses of her medical skills, prayers, kindness and belief that one person's darkness could be overcome with light.

To my mom's credit, her light (and will) shined strongly enough to win many times. And, often, those strays became beloved members of the Rouse House. For instance: "Rouse's Rabbit

Racer"—"Racer," for short—a rescued beaten beagle who became my best friend as a kid, sleeping on my pillow and sitting on the front of my inner tube, like a giant hood ornament, as we floated in the creek. Other times, my mom would take these animals to the local humane society or rescue shelter, and bug her friends, coworkers and county folk until they took that pet home.

There were, of course, times when it was too late. And those times haunted my mother. She believed deeply in the work of certain organizations—like hospice and The Humane Society of the United States (HSUS)—and gave generously to them. Working on behalf of those in need, on behalf of those who could not defend or help themselves, meant the world to her.

My entire life, as you can see, is the inspiration behind *I'm Not the Biggest Bitch in This Relationship*. And my mother's work is the reason I plan to direct a portion of my proceeds from this book to The Humane Society of the United States.

The Humane Society of the United States is described as the nation's largest animal-protection organization, backed by 11 million Americans. The HSUS works to reduce suffering and improve the lives of all animals by advocating for better laws; investigating animal cruelty; encouraging corporations to adopt animal-friendly policies; conducting animal rescue and disaster relief; and providing direct care for thousands of animals at their six centers for equines and wild animals, and through a program that provides free spay/neuter and wellness clinics to a number of impoverished communities that are without regular veterinary care. For more, I urge you to go to www.humanesociety.org

Most of the contributors to *Bitch* have local dog shelters, rescues and charities that are near and dear to their hearts—many of which they started on their own—and those are listed with their bios. I hope this anthology makes you take a closer look at their causes, your local animal shelters and rescue groups.

My mother also believed in the healing power of laughter. Erma Bombeck was our favorite writer. I always felt like I had two Midwestern moms looking over me, teaching the importance of humor in this world. It is what unites us. It is what keeps us sane.

A love of laughter and dogs: That is the uniting thread in *Bitch*. This book has truly been a labor of love, but one I realize has been worth it every time I kneeled down to hug my main mutts, Marge and Mabel, and their kisses warmed me, their smiles centered me, their love buoyed me.

Though we recently lost Marge, our nearly fourteen-year-old, eighty-pound Scooby-Doo mix, who saw me through five books and was truly my best friend, I realize she taught me more about faith, joy, hope and living in the moment than most people. Her sister, Mabel, our furry innocent and Labradoodle-beagle mix, has big paws to fill, but is already teaching me new wonders and filling my heart every day. And, one day soon, Gary and I will rescue another dog. In truth, that rescue will rescue us, and a long walk to new understandings will begin again. I cannot wait for that journey.

Unconditional love and laughter: Those are the gifts dogs bring us, and the beauty of this book.

So, enjoy! Laugh! And hug your dogs for me!

xx,

Wade

Acknowledgments

Thanks, first and foremost, to my mutts, Marge and Mabel. This book is because of you. (Although you really did none of the work, since you don't have opposable thumbs.) Thanks to my agent, Wendy Sherman, who loved the idea from day one, despite her first words being: "Ummm, Wade, do you know how much work an anthology involves?" I didn't. Do now. But so worth it. Thanks to my wonderful editor, Danielle Perez, who also loved this book (maybe even more than I did? Is that possible? Yes!) from day one, who loves dogs, and who worked tirelessly to make this a better book and an amazing experience. Thanks to everyone at NAL— from art to legal, to marketing, publicity and sales! You are a talented and driven team. Thanks to Jeff Wild of *Chelsea Lately* for all of his incredible help. Thanks to each and every contributor for responding to my insane queries, my endless follow-ups, my manic e-mails, and for writing such amazing pieces about dogs— current and past—that have changed your lives. I will forever be indebted to your kindness. You made me believe that there are not only good people in this world, but there are good people who happen to be writers, and, believe me, that is a rare thing indeed, I've learned. Thanks to Kathy Bauch at the Humane Society of the United States for her patience, kindness, support, and wonderful work. And, thanks to all of you, the people in this world who have opened their hearts, homes and wallets to rescues in need. Your light is making this world a brighter, barkier place. Finally, to Gary: I would not be here without you. I would not be me without you. I simply wouldn't be. And, neither would Marge or Mabel. And, my heartfelt apologies for continuing to scream, "SWEEET-IEEEE! Bring me some coffee!" Sorry, but I still think it's funny.

Wade Rouse, Editor

With work hailed by John Searles on NBC's *Today* show as "laugh-out-loud funny" and praised by *USA Today* as having "a wise, witty and often wicked voice," Wade Rouse is the critically acclaimed author of the memoirs *America's Boy*, *Confessions of a Prep School Mommy Handler*, and the bestselling *At Least in the City Someone Would Hear Me Scream: Misadventures in Search of the Simple Life*. His latest memoir, *It's All Relative: Two Families, Three Dogs, 34 Holidays, and 50 Boxes of Wine*, attempts to answer the question, "How come the only thing my family tree ever grows is nuts?" by looking at the yearly celebrations that unite us all and bring out the very best and worst in our nearest and dearest. Wade is a regular contributor to Michigan Public Radio and a humor columnist for *Metrosource* magazine. His essays have appeared in numerous national magazines and anthologies, including Forbes.com, Chicago Public Radio, Canadian Broadcasting's *Definitely Not the Opera*, and *The Customer Is Always Wrong: The Retail Chronicles*. Wade lives outside the resort town of Saugatuck, Michigan, where—between blizzards and beach weather—he writes and battles for bed space with his partner, Gary, and their mutt, Mabel. For more, visit www.WadeRouse.com, www.WadesWriters.com, or www.rhspeakers.com. Wade supports Wishbone Pet Rescue (www.wishbonepetrescue.com/wpr/) and Harbor Humane Society (www.harborhumane.org).